This book presented to:

_____

By:

_____

Park Avenue Christian Church
200 Years of
Seeking Justice
Embracing Diversity
Inspiring Imagination

John Wade Payne

John Payne (signature)

POLAR STAR PRESS

Park Avenue Christian Church: 200 Years of Seeking Justice, Embracing Diversity, and Inspiring Imagination.

For information, write Disciples of Christ Historical Society, 1101 19th Ave., S., Nashville, TN 37212

Polar Star Press, The Three Streams Cross (with *The Future of History*), and The Place History Calls Home are Trademarks of Disciples of Christ Historical Society, Nashville, Tennessee, USA, and Registered in the U.S. Patent and Trademark Office

Design by Kristin Russell

ISBN 978-0-9801966-5-8

12   24   17   72

Table of Contents

Publisher's Preface

It is not often that the history of a congregation is lived out so boldly. With Park Avenue Christian Church, however, the story unfolds in the city that was to become the center of the world. The setting itself lends the spectacular backdrop for the people and circumstances which formulated a variety of stories – and at the same time one, continuous story – that comprise the two hundred years of this historic church. If one word were to be chosen to describe this story, it would be *movement*. This is a congregation always on the move: from its many locations, to its dynamic leaders, and on to its forward vision. The reader will be treated in these pages to a Christian drama played out on a large stage, with all the appropriate props and costumes that make for intrigue from beginning to end.

And it is not often that a story is told so warmly. The narrative here is not delivered from the lectern, but one-on-one by a beloved former pastor of Park Avenue. This is a personal story conveyed personally, so that the hearer can indulge, along with the teller, in the legends which produced this now legendary church. Along with the author, we invite you to seek, to embrace, and to be inspired.

Polar Star Press
Nashville, Tennessee

Foreword

Seek the shalom of the city where I have sent you into exile, and pray to God on its behalf, for in its welfare you will find your welfare. (Jeremiah 29:7)

Time and again throughout the past 200 years, the message of the prophet has been made manifest in the congregation we know as the Park Avenue Christian Church (Disciples of Christ). From the faithful nine who met around a kitchen table in Lower Manhattan to today's growing numbers who gather on the Upper East Side to worship in the glorious sanctuary designed and modeled with inspiration from Sainte-Chapelle's in Paris, we have endeavored to bloom where we are planted in New York City, one of the greatest cities in the world! And to hear the call of the prophet in this time is to be a vital presence in this big, bustling, bodacious city.

Even more to hear the prophet's call is to claim the entire city as our parish. In doing so, we are provided amazing opportunities and significant challenges. A new chapter emerges. As we catch glimpses of living out our work here on the corner of 85th and Park Avenue, we are steeped in the story, the history, tradition, and courage of a people on whose shoulders we stand and about whom you will read in great detail in the pages to follow.

In this new chapter, we recognize that it is a rare New Yorker who is familiar with the Christian Church (Disciples of Christ) in the United States and Canada. Yet, many who cross our doorsteps find great resonance with a people who dare to proclaim "we have no creed but Christ, preach no Gospel but love, and have no purpose but to serve." We find that Disciples become a bridge in this increasingly interfaith and interreligious city and world. Many have searched far and wide for a Christian community that moves beyond the more commonplace conversations around diversity to that of *The Park's* declaration: "We are a Christian community that dares

3

to embrace the divinity of difference."

In this time, as in the time of the prophet, our well-being is inextricably linked to that of the city, we dare to do ministry in such a way that reaches and impacts the Upper East Side, the city of New York, and beyond with the radical claims of the Gospel of Jesus Christ. Indeed, we strive to build and to model the Beloved Community of God.

We find fresh evidence for the journey at every stop: From the voices of children in the Park Avenue Christian Church Day School, whose voices give us joy in their laughter and their songs; to the great energy, wit, and insight of 20 and 30 year olds (the XY Factor) who are teaching us about what it means to be Christian in the 21st century; to the outpouring of talent, commitment, and inspiration of the artistic community with which *The Park* is blessed; to the resurrected souls served each week at the Saturday Community Lunch Program; to those for whom recovery serves as a Lifeline; to the sage wisdom of the elders of today and times past.

It is with an overflowing abundance of pride, gratitude, and humility that I offer this Foreword to the account of our 200 year journey. For it is not often that we are blessed with the opportunity to celebrate a 200-year-old birthday! There are many who have made this possible.

First, I am pleased to offer profound gratitude to the Reverend John Wade Payne, author of this history, who has labored over the past year plus recording our story, and serving for twenty years as Senior Minister of the Park Avenue Christian Church. Also, special thanks go to Ima Jean Kidd, "ubiquitous elder" and "keeper" of the institutional memory of our congregation and to David Mitchell who serves with her as Co-Chair of the Bicentennial Celebration. Special appreciation is expressed to our entire Bicentennial Team, the Ministry Council, and all of the leaders and members past and present of our beloved congregation for their faithful, consistent and generous dedication over the years.

And of course this list would be incomplete without special kudos to my friends and valued colleagues: Glenn Carson, President; Sara Harwell, Chief Archivist; and the staff of Disciples of Christ Historical Society for making the publication of this history possible. Praise be to God for the wonderful work to which we have been called!

Søren A. Kierkegaard, the Danish theologian and philosopher, wrote that "life is lived forward, but understood backwards." And so even as we look back at a proud and glorious past, we press forward to a bright and inviting future of seeking justice, embracing diversity, and inspiring imagination.

Alvin O'Neal Jackson

Chapter 1

Seeking
The Church in the 19ᵗʰ Century

"It was my object to plead the cause of the oppressed."

— Pastor Urban Brewer

A New World and a New Church

Fervor and ferment defined the first decade of 19th century America. New York was a rapidly growing town of more than 80,000. The city was early known for its friendly welcome to newcomers. Noah Webster wrote in a letter on leaving town in 1788, "In point of sociability and hospitality, New York is hardly exceeded by any town in the U.S."

Energetic commerce was demonstrated by the fact that the largest employment was of cart men, moving goods and people. Manhattan traffic was becoming perilous. Cart men, livestock, horses, and wary pedestrians shared the dusty trash and offal-strewn roads (Broadway was one of the few paved streets).

The contrasts defining New York and the island of Manhattan were everywhere apparent. Washington Irving, who gave the city its "Gotham" nickname observed in 1809: "No sooner was the colony once planted, than like a luxuriant vine, it took root and throve amazingly." However, three decades later Henry David Thoreau would still quip, "The pigs in the street are the most respectable part of the population."

Religious temper was no less fevered. The legacies of Thomas Paine, and other free-thinking writers, had been influential, but the times had changed. The first years of the 19th century saw a whirlwind of itinerant evangelists at work in New York. The established churches of England and Scotland, Episcopal and Presbyterian, were gaining in membership, and impressive church buildings were being erected. In contrast, dissident Presbyterians, Baptists of many stripes, and Methodists were making headway, each convinced it had a monopoly on "true religion."

While the imported church traditions were thriving, challenges to the old order were brewing. In 1807 Thomas Campbell of the Old Light Anti-Burger Secessionist Presbyterian Church of Scotland immigrated and skirted New York on way to his missionary assignment in the Chartiers Presbytery on the Southwestern Pennsylvania frontier. The relationship was not a good fit, and Campbell soon found himself at odds with the leaders of the Presbytery. At issue were core doctrines, especially regarding the authority of faith as expressed in the Nicene and Apostolic Creeds, which he was convinced made assertions not supported by scripture. In addition, without the questioning of faith which often accompanied the assertions of 18th century rationalist philosophers, he had been influenced enough by them that he utterly refused to accept the claim that a "rise in one's emotional temperature" was required for salvation. Exasperation on both sides turned to rejection. The rigidity of his Presbytery barred him from offering Holy Communion to non-Presbyterian settlers when he was the only pastor for miles around. In 1809 he and the Presbytery parted ways. In response Campbell penned *The Declaration and Address,* challenging doctrines which separated Christians from one another in the new, expanding nation. Called by Disciples historians "a religious Magna Carta," the document embraced the ideal of freedom in the American constitution and applied it to the sectarian spirit of the established churches. His then radical objective was a vision of a united church freed from the dividing doctrines, creeds, and rituals which were separating Christian folk into often antagonistic clusters claiming exclusive divine origin for their interpretations of faith.

Two years later, Thomas's family, including his son Alexander, having left his studies at the University of Glasgow, arrived in America. Alexander enthusiastically embraced the energy of the new nation as he came ashore and upon his arrival in Pennsylvania discovered that he and his father had independently reached similar conclusions. Alexander had been attracted to the insights of Robert Sandeman and the Haldane brothers who were upsetting the established Presbyterian Church in Scotland. Convinced that the reformation spirit had lost its way, both father and son asserted that the church's future depended on re-instituting the church solely on New

Testament principles. Alexander had also read John Locke, which had led him further toward a more rational, perhaps even quasi-liberal, approach to faith. While he looked to scripture for the parameters of church structure and the Christian life, his biblical interpretations also sought the original context and setting of the words as well as their literal meaning. As Park Avenue Church's resident biblical scholar/elder Richard Sturm describes him:

> An excellent student of Latin and Greek, Campbell was a precursor of historical criticism and its methods of biblical interpretation that explore and honor a passage of Scripture in its original historical/literary/sociological/ theological context, before seeking to apply its message to our contemporary context. Campbell would also have us read each passage of Scripture with the whole Bible in mind, to avoid distortion or confusion in interpretation. Such study of the Word would bring the reader within what he called the 'understanding distance' of God, akin to the distance within which we can hear spoken words.

Thus, while seeds for the movement and denomination planted in this decade would not be immune to a literalistic interpretation, they would flower and undergird the halting but progressive growth of the congregation whose story is the subject of this book.

Alexander Campbell, as had his father, reluctantly forsook his Presbyterian associations. In 1811 they organized a new Christian community in Washington County, Pennsylvania, called the Brush Run Church and called themselves simply Disciples of Christ, one of the New Testament names for the early followers of Christ. They sought a new unity among the churches based solely on the New Testament, thus rejecting much of the nearly 2,000 years of sacred Christian tradition and history almost as if they were barnacles to be scraped off a buoy. They were not alone. Their plea for unity on these terms erupted throughout the United States and its territories, including Kentucky, where a revival and a movement for the unity of all Christians had already occurred under the leadership of Barton Warren Stone.

Ferment in Gotham

At the same time a similar restlessness was brewing 60 miles north from where young Alexander had come ashore, somewhere between the newly-completed, stately City Hall, and the Battery Promenade at the foot of Manhattan. The Ebenezer Baptist Church, meeting in Anthony Street (which became Worth Street in 1855), had already adopted some of the reformers' pleas, including weekly Communion and enhanced roles for elders. But to some perturbed members their approach to faith still reeked of the inflexibility of latter day Calvinism. These members had been quietly meeting to share their thoughts and questions about the "true nature" of the church. The subjects they pursued would later gladden Stone and the Campbells, father and son: questions about the nature of the churches established by those first followers of Jesus. Had the creeds and doctrines that evolved through the centuries moved the churches away from their New Testament roots? Was a new reformation demanded in this new nation?

Nine concerned members led by Ebenezer Church elder William Ovington and his wife Sarah crowded weekly into their home, 412 Greenwich Street, to engage these concerns. Today their address is subsumed in a parking garage near the new World Trade Center Tower 4. Then it was in the center of town, on one of its longest roads connecting New York north to Greenwich Village, still a day's carriage drive out in the country.

A near neighbor had been the popular Rickett's Equestrian Circus, which was closing to make way for one of the city's first attempts to offer culture to the public, the Greenwich Street Pantheon, built by the New York Academy of the Fine Arts. Their first exhibit was mostly plaster casts of the "great remains of antiquity" owned by the Louvre. While the Academy's Pantheon, never very successful, lasted only five years, the pious folks nearby at the Ovington home began their 200-year journey into history and the future's broadening way. After months of meetings for prayer, Bible study, and discussion, their fervor led them reluctantly but decisively to separate themselves from their Baptist roots. On an autumn Wednesday evening, October 10, 1810, their discussions and prayers finally were brought to fruition in a historic document which soon garnered twenty more signatures. This earnest group established the community which, after weekly "breaking bread and prayers" in more than ten locations with various names, 135 years later would establish their home for the past 65 years in the Park Avenue Christian Church (Disciples of Christ).

A facsimile copy of this document, given by Registry signer James Darsie's great-great-grandson, Hugh D. Darsie, hangs in the narthex of the church today. Although the possibility for women to assume leadership roles in the church was more than a century away, it seems significant that thirteen of the signers were female. From these humble beginnings in New York, and elsewhere, grew one of the largest religious bodies to be born in America, the Christian Church (Disciples of Christ).

This hardy little group and their descendants in faith will be the focus of this extraordinary New York story. In the beginning, services were held in various homes of the first nine signers of the Registry. Records indicate that quite soon the group was worshiping in space rented in one of the area's Watch Houses, all long-ago abolished forerunners of neighborhood police stations. It is thought that the church met in the Watch House at Hudson and Fulton Streets, but two others in the area are about as likely: at Wall and Broad Street, or at Chatham Square in Catherine Street.

In contrast to today's "revolving door" of church membership as people move in and out of the city, among the signers of the Registry are the names of those who are ancestors of the congregation's ministers and active members well into the 20th century. James and Ann Darsie were great-grandparents of John L. Darsie and great-great-grandparents of Hugh Darsie, both of whom served the congregation, John as pastor for nine months in 1908 and Hugh as student assistant in 1920. The Darsie family in all produced at least eleven ministers for the Disciples of Christ. Descendants of early member David Reid continued as members until the 1900s.

Signer Henry Errett, who acted as elder/pastor for fifteen years was tireless in his ministry to the fledgling "disciples of the Lord" congregation. Errett, before immigrating to New York from Arklow, Ireland, while a student and home for the holidays from the University of Dublin, witnessed the bloody assassination of his father, William Errett, a British army officer stationed in the south of Ireland, by a masked party of revolutionaries known for their "wearing of the green." The centuries-long enmity between Roman Catholics and Protestants in Ireland was in one of its severe stages, and Protestant William IV had posted William Errett in Ireland to help keep the peace. Henry's mother, Sarah Redmond Errett, was so traumatized by the shock of her husband's death that, after vain efforts to restore her mental health, Henry finally placed her in a retreat and sailed to America to begin again. Although he had been nurtured for ministry in the Baptist Church of Scotland, he soon achieved success as a New York real estate agent and found a home for his religious sympathies in the meetings at the Ovington home on Greenwich Street. There he met and courted young Sophia Kemmish, one of the original nine signers of the October 1810 Registry. Errett joined the new congregation and they were married the next June, likely the church's first wedding. The couple had six children, one of whom, Isaac Errett, was the first publisher and editor of the *Christian Standard*, which remains a major periodical of the movement.

Immediately recognized for his leadership abilities at only 23 years of age, Henry Errett led the congregation (sharing the work with William Ovington) until his early death in 1825. They eschewed the titles "reverend" or "minister" but simply called themselves "elder" or "teacher" and suggested that the congregation call itself by the biblical "Disciples of Christ."

Henry Errett was a key figure in bringing the Disciples of Christ in New York together with the movement headed by Alexander Campbell. Errett wrote numerous tracts which were widely read and brought some measure of recognition to the congregation. One, entitled "An Essay on the Order and Discipline of the Apostolic Churches," was published in 1811 and widely distributed. For about three months in 1820 the fiery evangelist for the movement, Walter Scott, was part of the fledgling New York congregation before moving westward and spurring phenomenal growth for the young movement. In 1820 Scott discovered Errett's pamphlet on the nature of baptism which he shared with Alexander Campbell. To both men Errett offered an eye-opening description of baptism beyond simply being a biblical requirement for new Christians. Errett's position that baptism is key "to the remission of sins" was never a universally held position among free-thinking Disciples, but it did inspire Scott and Campbell with a deeper appreciation for the sacred baptismal experience. Henry Errett and his son Isaac were key leaders of the Disciples of Christ, which in a few decades would become the fastest growing American religious movement in the 19th century. Undoubtedly this little congregation is among the earliest, continuing Disciples communities. While *The New York Times* in the 19th century consistently referred to the congregation as the "oldest" church in the movement, the Disciples congregation in Harrodsburg,

Kentucky, looks to a beginning in 1803 and continues to serve today.

In 1831 Alexander Campbell visited the New York congregation and found divisions brewing over church order. Various conflicts had simmered for decades as these reformers sought a firm New Testament pattern for church order. He was able to bring reconciling unity to the differing parties, while often speaking to large audiences of both Christians and skeptics in the famous Tammany Hall and Concert Hall. In days long before sound-bites, it was recalled that he kept audience attention for two hours, and more.

It was probably on this visit that Campbell celebrated communion with the congregation on a small, undistinguished table that was long a treasured artifact of the church. Today, it is in the collection held by Disciples of Christ Historical Society.

Acting as ministers, presiding elders Henry Errett and William Ovington were unpaid volunteers. Together with Alexander Campbell, they at first rejected a salaried clergy as not part of the New Testament experience which they sought to emulate. Intent on gaining new members for their newly reformed congregation, these elders widely distributed a circular letter from "a church in Christ in the City of New York, the one organized in 1810," seeking to locate similar groups across the United States and Canada. The letter reveals the nature of the congregation's life and work: the order of worship, hymn singing, weekly Lord's Supper, scripture reading, prayers, exhortation by the elders, and statements of praise for previous accomplishments. It was signed by William Ovington and Henry Errett, elders, and deacons Jonathan Hatfield, James Saunders, and Benjamin Hendrickson. The letter received even wider distribution when Alexander Campbell reprinted it in his monthly periodical, *The Christian Baptist* (August 6, 1827).

Uptown Journey Begins

By 1817 the church was worshiping regularly in Sullivan Street, where a farm once owned by the family of the early Dutch merchant and reformer Nicholas Bayard, whose name and land morphed into "Bowery," was being developed into row houses near today's Sullivan Street Playhouse. During the first decade the congregation grew to 80 and gradually moved north as New York expanded uptown. From 1831 to 1837 the congregation, now called "The Primitive Christian Church of Disciples," worshiped at St. John's Lane and York Street, where their neighbor was the handsome St. John's Episcopal Chapel built in 1803, now demolished. Once impressive and the home of Alexander Hamilton, these short Tribeca streets west of Sixth Avenue are today lined with windowless warehouses.

By 1837 the congregation had grown to about 150 members and moved to a small building constructed by church member Eleazor Parmleyon on his property at 80 Greene Street, between Spring and Broome Streets. It remained there until 1850. This building too was long ago demolished, the address now being the location of art galleries and a Swedish mattress company housed on the ground floors of a late 19th century, six-story, cast-iron building. As it grew, the congregation became increasingly aware that their life and work could not be sustained only by elder-pastors receiving little or no compensation. A new era was dawning as the 19th century reached its midpoint.

New York, which had been the country's largest city for decades, was burgeoning. The first barges sailed the Erie Canal in 1825 and opened a water highway for New York's goods and services far to the west. Between 1830 and 1850, 200,000 people moved into the city, which now numbered more than 515,000. Many observed then as now, "The business of New York is business." Captain Frederick Marryat wrote in *A Diary in America* in 1837, "I have never seen any city so admirably adapted for commerce."

Up to this time the city had been primarily middle class and was 95 percent of American-born parentage. Its crafts workers were excellent, and its banking and commercial businesses were becoming dominant in the country. The city's leaders were Protestant entrepreneurs and the city was run primarily and amazingly by volunteers. But all was not well. A major New York enterprise was investing in the slave trade, and the growing abolition movement was not well received by the bankers and business interests. At least half the homes in the city still had no sewers or paved streets. Into this environment the Irish depression and potato famine brought thousands of unskilled Catholics who disembarked into New York City between 1840 and 1850. This tsunami of immigration changed the population to one-quarter Irish, mostly illiterate and unskilled. For the first time government institutions, including the police and fire departments, and public schools were established. Civic groups and the Catholic Church opened hospitals, but the fast-paced social change was beyond volunteer leadership. Competing ethnic tensions and rising crime opened the way to the machine politics of the next decades.

It was in the midst of this social earthquake that the little Church of the Disciples in 1850 achieved the stability of incorporation and purchased a building for its congregation's home at the cost of $10,500. Over the door of their new home at 70 – 72 West 17th Street just east of Sixth Avenue was the inscription "Disciples' Meeting House," the designation preferred by Alexander Campbell. A few blocks from Union Square, the space today would occupy only a small portion of a red-brick, contemporary office/residential tower. Although New York City had increased by hundreds of thousands, the church grew slowly.

As the congregation of 174 settled into their new home they ambitiously called their first regular pastor, Dr. Silas E. Shepard, who was also a practicing homeopathic physician and had previously served a similar congregation in Troy, New

York. His involvement in the restoration of "New Testament Christianity" was already established. Earlier Dr. Shepard had published a monthly periodical, *The Primitive Christian* from 1835 to 1841. He is also remembered for his controversial "scathing rebuke" concerning alleged cruelties in the Auburn, New York prison in a series entitled "The Prison Chronicles." Serving the congregation for six years, he was remembered in typical 19th century rhetoric by M. O. Tiers: "Dr. Shepard's imposing personal presence, his mental power and culture, his correct diction, well-modulated voice and familiarity with the various original languages of classical and sacred literature, secured attention to his pulpit ministrations, and so we obtained a better hearing in the city." He resigned in 1856 after a call to a church in Troy, Pennsylvania, where he died in 1876.

Two brief pastorates followed that of Dr. Shepard. The first, by D.L. Burnett, about whom little is known, lasted less than a year. He was followed by the energetic and charismatic J. Carroll Stark, a young Tennessean in his twenties, who came following his sophomore year at Hiram College. In addition to his brief pastorate of less than two years, he went on to serve congregations in seven states. He is chiefly remembered today for his involvement in the controversies which would split the Disciples of Christ from the Churches of Christ in the early years of the 20th century. Increasingly heated issues concerning whether church organizations and worship practices must be based on only what could be literally verified from the New Testament found a major focus in the debate over whether "the word of God permitted the use of instruments of music for praise in the church of Jesus Christ." In 1903 in Hendersonville, Tennessee, Stark, in a well attended and widely publicized four-day debate, argued for the use of instruments against Joe W. Warlick. Park Avenue Church today, so committed to instrumental as well as vocal music and all of the arts, should honor and express gratitude for Stark's contribution to what now may seem strangely quaint, but then was a hot issue among these latter-day reformers. As will be detailed later, in 1920 these differences finally concluded as a portion of the 1810-founded congregation went their separate ways to establish the Manhattan Church of Christ, today a nearby Upper Eastside neighbor and partner in the Park Avenue Church's Community Lunch Program.

Issues such as these were reflected in the rather rigid discipline maintained in the early years of the congregation. Delinquent members were sent reprimands. Others were dismissed for non-attendance or for not contributing financially. One woman was tried for "falsehood and slandering the church, contention and lack of Christian spirit." She resigned and the minutes reported that she "went out from us as not of us."

The 1850s saw changes accelerating in the city. Tammany, an Irish, immigrant-supported, Democratic Party political machine would come to dominate the city's politics for decades. Civic minded, "old money" merchants campaigned for a Central Park, and a design competition for the park began in 1857. Designed by Frederick Law Olmstead, Manhattan's Central Park would become the first and one of the most magnificent landscaped parks in an American city and the inspiration for the now-uptown congregation's sobriquet "The Park" in recent years.

Let Justice Roll

New York's strong commercial ties to the South and its large, struggling, and mostly poor immigrant population exacerbated divisions concerning the abolition of slavery. Over 80 percent of American-grown cotton was shipped overseas out of the city's harbor. These tensions culminated in the four-day Draft Riots in June 1863 over resistance to military conscription during the Civil War. Several churches were incendiary-bombed for advocating abolition. Fires burned throughout the city; property was destroyed and racist hostilities erupted.

Into the midst of this agitation a 23-year-old graduate in law from the University of the City of New York and from the recently-established Union Theological Seminary, Urban Cooper Brewer, was called to the ministry of the congregation in 1860. Now sometimes named the Christian Chapel as well as First Church of the Disciples, the community began tentatively to explore a justice-oriented, progressive stance which would grow significantly in the years ahead. Urban Brewer was a pioneer contributor.

The respect accorded Urban Brewer and the enhanced reputation he brought to the congregation was underscored by his appointment to give the law commencement address, entitled "Shoddy Patriotism," on May 7, 1862 to the University of the City of New York. Published in booklet form, his opposition to Americans' tendency to nationalistic bias was widely distributed. The recognition of his ministry was affirmed by his appointment to the Board of Managers of Alexander Campbell's periodical, *The Millennial Harbinger,* in 1864 and later as a board member of the American Bible Union.

Undoubtedly his finest achievement during his New York ministry was his effort in support of the abolition of slavery. In an environment where the slavery question was deemed divisive and controversial, many of the city's clergy sought to distance themselves from the risky political and social upheavals around them. But this was not Urban Brewer's approach. Uncertain of his congregation's sympathies, he nevertheless scheduled a cutting-edge lecture to be held at the Christian Chapel on Sunday evening, January 4, 1863. Entitled "The Bible and American Slavery: A Discourse," the topic generated a full house. Afterwards, in doubt about his congregation's response, he offered to resign. That same month he received a letter from a committee appointed at the church's annual meeting requesting that the church be permitted to publish the address and stated:

[We have] the earnest desire and firm conviction that principles advocated by you in that address should be widely disseminated throughout the land, being illustrative, as they are, of some of the evils resulting from an *'Institution'* embracing in its usage the most revolting, wicked, and infamous crimes – the most inhuman and atrocious cruelties – the most heinous and flagrant sins, that ever disgraced, degraded, or debased humanity, or ruined a nation. We are dear sir, respectfully and cordially, Eleazar Parmly, Francis Duncan, Abraham A. Andruss, Alvah Hall, William D. Stewart.

Obviously the members' primary commitment to the restoration of New Testament Christianity had been expanded to take on the "principalities and powers."

Brewer replied: "It was my object, in the discourse which asks in terms so complimentary, to vindicate the Bible and plead the cause of the oppressed. If publication will subserve the interests of truth and enslaved humanity, I most willingly comply with your request." The lecture was printed and widely distributed. Yet somehow for over a century it was lost to the congregation's records. Thankfully, it found its way through a legacy to Cornell University and quietly lay in their library's archives. Rediscovered, it is now a revered part of the University's Samuel J. May Anti-Slavery Collection and has recently been republished in book form as a significant contribution to the history of the abolitionist movement in the United States.

While the 30-page lecture is too lengthy to include here, a brief summary and quotation follow. The address opens with an affirmation of the "Bible doctrine of the unity and universal brotherhood of the human race" and includes a survey of slavery since the Greek and Roman empires. Brewer develops a careful exposition of various New Testament references in which he passionately refutes with biblical quotations those who seek to support slave ownership and trade. He concludes by referring to Abraham Lincoln's Emancipation Proclamation:

> The National Executive, inspired by a lofty moral courage, which will make his name immortal, has pronounced an edict for the expulsion of this monster of iniquity. Shall that edict be sustained by a Christian people? Shall it find an echo in the sanctuary of God, or shall the hand go back on the dial of human progress, and we relapse into the darkness of barbarism? . . . A great day of wrath has come. The Armageddon of oppression is being fought, and a continent is the battlefield. . . . O! People of God! Arise in the majesty and might of your heaven-given strength, put on the whole armor of truth, and go forth with weapons of celestial temper to meet this boasting adversary. . . . When the nation is educated to do justice and love mercy; to give freedom to the oppressed, and to know that God rules in the kingdoms of men, then will that great Arbiter of national destiny cause His face to shine upon us, and the 'garments rolled in blood' will pass away.

The congregation gained recognition for its stance and leadership. Brewer was deeply respected and loved, and records show that his salary was raised annually. The congregation was resolute in its commitment to the end of slavery in America although it would be over forty years before the congregation would include black members. Nevertheless, the church had begun its journey toward a socially responsible commitment to the gospel and a growing progressive model among the churches.

On a more ecclesiastical topic, in 1867 Brewer published

another booklet addressing a long-standing concern: "Ought the Church to Wear a Human Name?" referring to the Disciples' avoidance of non-biblical denominational titles such as Methodist, Presbyterian, and the like.

Although this was still a period when in many churches it was considered unseemly for women to assume positions of leadership or even speak in meetings, the Civil War opened new roles for them. The May 5, 1862 minutes of the Dorcas Society recorded that the women of the Christian Chapel, First Church of the Disciples were "taking immediate steps for relief of the sick and wounded soldiers now arriving in the city from the seat of the war." The minutes of April 19, 1865 also reveal that the women of the church were actively involved in "Services being held in the church during the burial service in Washington of our lamented President of the United States, Abraham Lincoln." However, women were still virtually silent in the church's boards and committees. The regular reports of the Dorcas Society and the later Ladies Aid Society were always read by a man. Finally in 1873 six deaconnesses were elected, but ballots were only distributed among male church members.

More Ups and Downs

In the midst of this turbulent decade the congregation moved in 1865. Selling their 17th Street building, they purchased another at 26 – 28 West 28th Street near Broadway for $42,000. Their new setting had been built in 1860 by the Free Will Baptists. Today only a remnant of its original Romanesque facade and entrance remains and can be seen only by careful observation from the street, but the building's checkered history is worth noting. When the church moved again in 1883, the building was purchased by James Everard, who converted it into the Turkish, Roman and Electric Baths. Well known and still operating in

1977, it was the scene of a devastating fire that claimed nine lives. It now houses a handbag wholesaler and a microprocessor business.

Urban Brewer's New York ministry continued until 1869, when he was called to Indiana where he served in Indianapolis, Greensburg, and Danville well into the 20th century. Following Urban Brewer, W. J. Howe was pastor for one year, C. C. Foote for two, and W. C. Dawson for two more beginning in January, 1873. Encouraging more congregational participation in worship, Dawson introduced responsive readings of the scripture, but this was soon abandoned because of resistance by the members. His suggestion that they officially adopt the name, "Disciples of Christ," was approved and has remained part of the congregation's name ever since.

Next came D. R. Van Buskirk, from Bentonville, Indiana, in December 1874, about whom *The New York Times* reported that "among the members of the church, he is held in the highest esteem." That same article pointed out that the Disciples have "only one congregation in this city. Throughout the Western States, however, the denomination is very strong, and it has built colleges in Kentucky, Ohio, Iowa, Illinois, Missouri, and other states. In the last census its entire membership was given at 600,000, its comparative numerical strength being recorded as "No. 4." What was meant by "No. 4" can only be surmised: the fourth largest? Not likely.

The church was thriving with a Sunday School of 300. Lay leadership was strong, led by Robert Christie, who "held every office" in the congregation and Herman Nesslage, who served simultaneously as elder, trustee, and chorister. Each was much beloved by the members, and their descendants were active in the congregation through the 1960s.

One member's recorded memory hints that piety was not all that was on the minds of worshipers who apparently tolerated long-windedness unimaginable today. Goings on at the nearby Fifth Avenue Theatre elicited this comment: "All church services were continued during the summer and when the doors and windows were open during the weekly prayer meetings, I have a guilty remembrance of listening to the soft music of the orchestra from the theatre instead of 'inclining mine ear' to some dear brother's lengthy prayer." A later recorded memory reported the purchase of a clock for $1.25, which was placed, for obvious reasons, on the pulpit facing the preacher.

When *The New York Times* reported Dr. Van Buskirk's resignation on March 14, 1879, it was stated that "his reasons for giving up his charge here arise solely from the desire of himself and family to return to their old home in Bentonville, Indiana, where Dr. Van Buskirk will resume his connection with the church in which he preached immediately after his ordination."

Standing on the Promise

The congregation looked to Louisville for a new pastor, Joseph Bradford Cleaver. Scholarly, well-educated, and biblically-literate, he especially brought growth and depth to the Sunday School and mid-week services. Evolving, the congregation was shedding its independent, anti-establishment-church past. The two principles on which the Disciples were founded, the cry for unity and cooperation among the churches, were gradually beginning to take precedence over the notion of a literal restoration of primitive New Testament Christianity. Joseph Cleaver's gregarious openness and popularity contributed to the change.

A story from *The New York Times* of January 22, 1880, reflects the positive mood throughout the congregation. Headlined "A Novel Church Fair," the report describes a picturesque and very successful Knickerbocker kitchen festival and fair offered to the community. It was sponsored by the church's Society of Cheerful Givers, designed by Miss Ana B. P. Hall, and carried out by members of the society including Pastor Cleaver. The Sunday School was transformed into "a Knickerbocker dining room complete with a great fireplace and most inviting dining tables. Young ladies of the church clad in rich, old-fashioned costumes dispensed delicacies to their guests." The article concluded that the same group planned a "Martha Washington Tea Party" the next month.

Shortly thereafter the church received more renown, participating in the city's excitement and honor in receiving an ancient obelisk, sometimes called "Cleopatra's Needle," from the government of Egypt. Pastor Cleaver was invited to represent the congregation, and as chaplain of the Grand Lodge of Masons of the State of New York, he offered the dedicatory benediction for the public ceremony, the laying of the obelisk's foundation in Central Park west of the Metropolitan Museum of Art.

Members were delighted when Pastor Cleaver announced his engagement to Elizabeth Stronach, whose father was one of the congregation's elders, and mother was president of the Dorcas Society. Their wedding was a major celebration for the members and their marriage enriched the fellowship.

Increases in membership encouraged the congregation to begin contemplating the purchase of property on which to begin their own building program. One can perhaps imagine what would have been the outcome if the congregation had accepted their first plan — a proposition in 1880 to buy four lots and build their new church on Park Avenue and 82nd Street, only three blocks from where Park Avenue Church is located today. "Not expedient at this time" was the conclusion, and probably it was a bit too far uptown in a growing, but still rather sparsely-settled German community called Yorkville. However, in less than two years they sold the 28th Street building for $100,000 and began to construct their first new church building at 321 – 325 West 56th Street, three blocks south of Columbus Circle, just west of Eighth Avenue.

Dublin-born, Irish-American architect Charles Mettam ("highly distinguished" according to *The New York Times* and also architect of the landmark New York Historical Society building) designed an imposing and "substantial" brick Romanesque church. Mettam is also remembered for his prescience as the first to suggest a workable design for New York's "El," the elevated Third Avenue commuter train of bygone days. The church's location is now the site of the eye-catching, cross-hatched, tower addition to the venerable Hearst building.

The cornerstone was laid on May 29, 1883, in a celebration that included well-known Disciples and congregation leaders, H. King Pendleton (temporary pastor), A. A. Andrus, O. H. Bartholomew, and A. B. Chamberlain. Inside the cornerstone was placed a list of ministers from 1850 to 1883, a report on the Sunday School by Robert Christie, a brochure by Isaac Errett (son of founding member Henry Errett) on the nature of the Disciples of Christ, and copies of the *Christian-Evangelist* and Isaac Errett's *Christian Standard*. Another item underscored the missionary priority of 19th century Protestants to convert the world to Christianity: a pamphlet in which John 3:16 was printed in the 174 languages into which the Bible had so far been translated. This date has long been celebrated as a red-letter day in New York. U.S. President Chester A. Arthur and New York Governor Grover Cleveland were both in town to mark the date. Nine hundred bicyclists and 1,700 police paraded down Fifth Avenue in front of 10,000 spectators. Did they note the cornerstone laying? Perhaps, if they glanced at the half-dozen lines in the newspapers. This was the day when people around the world marveled at the opening of the up-to-that-time largest ever suspension span — the Brooklyn Bridge over the East River.

City, Church, Challenge

The Disciples congregation, proud of their growth and their new home, continued to be a primarily Anglo enclave while the rate of immigration from southern Europe grew rapidly around them. To and through New York, millions journeyed in hope. In recognition France presented the city with the beloved copper-clad Statue of Liberty in 1886. Emblazoned on its interior pedestal is a more altruistic message than many New Yorkers would have embraced: Emma Lazarus's poem which concludes, "Give me your tired, your poor, your huddled masses yearning to breathe free, the wretched refuse of your teeming shore. Send these, the homeless, tempest-tost to me, I lift my lamp beside the golden door!"

Social upheaval was inevitable. While middle-class Protestantism would provide *noblesse oblige* charity and partisan handouts, it would seek to distance itself from the poverty of the masses exploited by the corrupt political machine of Tammany Hall. This was the age of the "robber barons" of banking and industry. Heavy-handed policing sought to stem the ever-present revolutionary spirit among the poorly-paid workers. Reformers were fiercely repressed. Some of the relief burden was picked up by the churches, especially those of an evangelical nature, but the charity was never adequate to the need. It was an era when the emphasis was on helping only the "deserving poor," and the going political view was that charity would only increase pauperism. Only in the last quarter of the century did the community begin to consider poverty as a social challenge instead of solely an individual problem.

The Disciples congregation made efforts toward helping the poor, but it also had its own on-going internal challenges. While it never lost a building or faced bankruptcy, as did scores of New York churches in this and later times, there were seasons when pastors received a reduced salary. Church operations were funded in the 19th century primarily by pew rents. In 1865 the trustees authorized the "pew committee" to raise the rents to meet the expense of increasing the pastor's salary. Meeting resistance, two years later they adopted a plan which was a preview of today's voluntary "pledges" or "estimates of giving." For awhile no offerings were received at the Sunday evening services, but in 1871 they were resumed, and because of the dire need, devoted entirely to the "poor fund," which was never adequately supported. A report from 1876 reveals the ever-present dilemma: only 40 out of a membership of 270 had contributed anything.

Over the arched, Romanesque entrance to their new home uptown on 56th Street the name read First Church, Disciples of Christ. Their new pastor, Benjamin Bushrod Tyler, would become the longest serving to that time – from 1883 to 1895. While much of the city around them was in turmoil, the congregation enjoyed increased growth and stability. The membership of more than 350 had obligated themselves for $105,000 for their new sanctuary, Sunday school, and offices. In addition the congregation maintained a home for their pastor and his family.

B. B. Tyler, as he was called, was 43 when he arrived in New York after serving the well-established First Christian Church of Louisville, Kentucky. Accepting a call to New York from a thriving, substantial, Midwestern congregation to serve the relatively small Gotham church was to become a recurring pattern in the ensuing years. At its best the New York church offered both pastor and congregation formidable challenges and an increased measure of esteem, influence, and visibility.

Born into an Illinois Disciples family, Tyler early determined to become a minister, but after two years at nearby Eureka College, the Civil War interrupted his studies. From that time on he was self-educated. At Eureka he met and later on Christmas Day in 1882 married Sarah Burton. Sarah was as active in the mission of the church as her husband was. It was written of Tyler that "he is the most popular preacher among us." Even a partial list of his accomplishments is impressive: Board of Managers of the American Bible Society, President of the Chautauqua Union of New York, and the Christian Endeavor Union (an ecumenical youth organization predating the denominationally-based youth fellowships). He was also elected President of the major interdenominational Protestant Christian education effort of the time, the International Sunday School Convention. His published writings include a 595-page *History of the Disciples of Christ* (1894), a widely-read series of sermons preached in New York entitled "The Way of Salvation," and a weekly "New York Letter" column for ten years in *The Christian Standard*. He was awarded an honorary Doctor of Divinity by Drake University in 1891. Tyler's comment on Abraham Lincoln has been republished in numerous collections of quotations. He concluded that Lincoln's "last public utterances show forth the confidence and the fire of an ancient Hebrew prophet."

Sarah Tyler's activities in New York were as energetic as her husband's. During these years Jacob Riis's challenges to the social-fabric were gaining visibility. A young Danish immigrant, Riis at first survived only by living on the streets. He finally found work as a reporter with *The New York Tribune*. Proud of his success, he thought of himself as a self-made man and wrote, "As to the man who will not work, let him starve." Inevitably, his new job opened his eyes to the grim realities of slum life. He wrote that these sights "gripped my heart until I felt that I must tell them, or burst." His news reports and his embrace of the new wonder of flash photography spotlighted the squalor and tugged at his readers' hearts and minds. Riis's misery-revealing journalism and the social gospel preaching of reformers such as Walter Rauschenbusch were beginning to impact New York churches.

Sarah Tyler heard and acted creatively to meet these challenges. With the able support of the women of the church she organized a large sewing school in the church basement so that young women could learn to be self-supporting. Successful as she was in attracting pupils to the school, the efforts were daunting and frustrating. Seamstresses, when they could find employment, worked mainly in sweatshops that paid little more than a dollar for a day's work of 16 hours. Macy's paid $1.50 a day to saleswomen who were never allowed to sit down and were simply dismissed after a few years lest they ask for a raise. Knowing of little she could do to mitigate their misery, and aware that the poor had scant experience in managing the meager money they received, she then created the unique "Penny Provident Fund," an educational program to train children of poverty in habits of thrift. She also served as president of the ecumenically-supported, charity-driven Christian Woman's Board of Missions for the state of New York. Late in life, commenting appreciatively on her husband's ministries, she nevertheless quipped, "He speaks. I work!"

As the couple completed their years in New York, Tyler's health deteriorated. To recover, they traveled extensively, including to Egypt. Later B. B. Tyler served the South Broadway Church in Denver and often preached on a topic he called "Didactic Evangelism" to large, enthusiastic audiences throughout the Midwest. He died in 1922.

As interim pastor W. C. Morse, one of the ministers from nearby Calvary Baptist Church, served briefly in a part-time capacity. In 1897 another minister began a short interim and he would later become one of the outstanding Christian scholars of his time — Edward Scribner Ames. Born in Eau Claire, Wisconsin in 1870, he was the son of a Disciples minister who served congregations in several Midwestern towns. After completing studies at Drake University, he continued at Yale University Divinity School. He first preached at New York's First Church of Disciples of Christ in 1893, at the invitation of B. B. Tyler. After receiving his degrees, marrying, and completing his Ph.D. at the University of Chicago, he returned to New York and served the Disciples congregation as interim pastor for three months (April – June), preaching twice each Sunday. This brief tenure notwithstanding, he left a significant legacy with the people. Late in his life Dr. Ames wrote of his short New York ministry: "The three months I spent with you in 1897 are vivid in my memory." He remembered one he called "a valiant hero" among the elders, A. A. Andrus, of whom he wrote, "His life alone would have made it a sacred place. During the past twenty years how many have been strengthened there against temptation and inspired to holy deeds." Dr. Ames served as dean of the Disciples Divinity House and pastor of sister congregation University Church of Disciples of Christ in Chicago from 1900 to 1940. His well-received books reflected his strong liberal Christian commitments. The warm reception Dr. Ames received from the congregation for his humanistic approach to theology offers a further glimpse of the changes occurring within a significant portion of the community.

In recent years other Disciples congregations had been established in the city. Among them the Lenox Church DOC and the Second Church DOC in the Bronx. Dr. Ames, knowing of a group already established in Chicago, envisioned a partnership of these congregations and the formation of an association "for the study and advancement of the distinctive principles of the Disciples." Through the efforts of Ames, Robert Christie, and J. J. Philputt of First Church, a Disciples Club of 27 members of the three congregations was formed. Out of these beginnings the Disciples Union of New York and vicinity was formed in 1901. The group's agenda included promoting social, educational, spiritual, and evangelistic interests of Disciples in the area. A. U. Chaney, A. E. McBee, and E. M. Bowman represented First Church. The association would continue its work for decades and become a significant part of the restructured Northeastern Region of the Christian Church (Disciples of Christ) in the 1960s.

Wallace C. Payne, who had been pastor of the Third Church Disciples of Christ in Philadelphia for five years, began his ministry at First Church in New York on New Year's Day, 1889. He had preached in 1886 at the invitation of B. B. Tyler, and while not seeking a new charge, had so impressed the congregation that he was sought out after Tyler's resignation. Payne was a native Ohioan, educated at Bethany College and at Yale Divinity School. Anticipating his arrival *The New York Times* reported: "He has done important work there (Philadelphia), adding some 400 members to his church and doubling the attendance in the Sunday School, so a new and larger church has become necessary. Mr. Payne is a fluent speaker with a pleasing full-toned voice, and it is said that his manner in the pulpit is easy and his style of preaching practical and direct."

While few details are recorded about Payne's ministry, the *Times* reported that within days after he arrived he was elected secretary of a group of some of the most prominent Protestant pastors in New York, including a delegation of members of the First Church of Disciples and representatives of Marble Collegiate Church and others to usher in a "Crusade Against Saloons." Seeking legislation to prohibit alcoholic beverages in the city, the group called itself the "New York Prohibition Union." Their motto was: "In the name of Jesus Christ the King, the liquor traffic must die!" The temperance movement blamed nearly all of society's ills on the consumption of alcoholic beverages. For the next quarter century the prohibition issue obsessed not only New York, but the nation. Virtually all of the Protestant clergy in New York City supported legislation which in 1920 became the law of the land for 13 years with the passage of the 18th amendment to the U.S. Constitution.

The new 20th century saw no abatement in New York's relentless growth. The pace and social upheaval of immigration never faltered; only the nationalities changed. Construction of the first subway was tunneling under Lexington Avenue and began hauling passengers up and down the East Side in 1904. A society-changing event focused the city on the sad truth that it often takes tragedy to bring attention to deliberately created cruel and unsafe working conditions. One wonders whether any of the young women so thoughtfully trained by Sarah Tyler and the church's volunteers became victims on March 25, 1911 in the Triangle Shirtwaist Factory fire in Greenwich Village which, because all exits were locked, trapped and took the lives of 146 garment workers.

Chapter 2

Embracing
The Church in the 20th Century

"Christianity lives by adventure."

— Pastor Finis Idleman

Loyalty's Ambiguities

In 1899 the first issues of the church periodical *Forward* began weekly publication and continues as an expanded, welcomed monthly today. Its combined New Testament restoration and future oriented title was inspired by the Apostle Paul's comment in Philippians 3:13: "**Forward** to the things which are before." Fortunately, nearly all issues have been preserved in the Park Avenue archives serve as a major source of information in the congregation's history. An interesting sidelight is to note various paid advertisements which appeared in its first decades of publication. One promised, "No dust, No disease when the house is cleaned with a Richmond Suction Cleaner!" Culture was offered: "Mrs. Florence E. Stinson will give a thorough course in ELOCUTION, deep breathing, voice development, coaching of plays." Church members, too, offered their services: "Robert Christie and son, carpenters and builders. Jobbing promptly attended to."

That same year the Disciples congregation sought another pastor. In almost every congregation a scandal will sometime punctuate its history as did the one that arose during the pastorate of Benjamin Q. Denham. Installed in September, 1899, Mr. Denham had grown up on a farm in Bloomington, Illinois, and was educated at Illinois Wesleyan University. Serving congregations in Kansas City and North Tonawanda, New York, he was said to have brought 1,300 converts into the church. A similar growth began immediately as he began his New York ministry. By 1902 the services were so well attended that ushers asked members to "give up their (own) pews to visitors" and sit elsewhere. That same year the trustees were so impressed with his leadership that he was given leave to take an extended trip to Europe. The choir increased in numbers so that one of the church's first concerts was offered in 1903. On the 20th anniversary of the occupation of the church building, September 1, 1905, a major celebration was planned with letters of commendation from across the nation.

Social justice issues continued to be addressed as Pastor Denham included concern for "conditions prevailing among the southern Negroes" in his preaching and writing. And he emphasized the congregation's embrace of a breadth of faith remarkable for its time. "We are not indifferent as to what a man believes regarding the future life, punishment of sin, etc. But we refer any and all disciples to the New Testament for the necessary teaching. . . . No one is forced or required to understand those teachings in the same way others do. . . There is a wide holding of individual opinion among our members."

His dramatic, even charismatic, preaching was clever and pious-sounding. However, he became involved with a series of moral issues and accusations which divided the congregation and ultimately required the courts to clarify and settle. Although one church member would assert that the church "prospered and grew as never before," the next few years saw tensions mount and divisions multiply for and against his ministry.

In an acerbic letter to *The New York Times* responding to a December 1900 editorial which he felt was unduly sympathetic to a comment by a Chicago pastor that, "Unless the church become a continual vaudeville it cannot hold its congregation," Denham wrote, "Must the church conform to the world to live?. . . What is the real value of large numbers? It is not entertainment, but that men may be led to become genuine followers of Christ!" He continued at great length chastising the editorial writers for "conforming to the world spirit instead of contesting it." An interesting letter, since the record indicates that Mr. Denham was indeed an entertaining, charismatic, emotionally-stimulating preacher and perhaps even "vaudevillian" since he was described as "hip-swinging" by one pew sitter.

While his preaching engendered loyalty among many of the members, his moral integrity was not beyond question. Church member for 43 years, Mrs. Elizabeth B. Grannis, self-styled "radical" suffragette and president of The National Christian

League for Promotion of Purity, bitterly and publicly accused pastor Denham of immoral and indecent behavior, a charge which had been made but unproven in his previous pastorates. Given the changing social mores of the time, especially concerning women's role in the church, the controversy proved destructive well beyond the facts. Newspapers from Maine to California eagerly publicized the fracas. *The New York Times* reported that a congregational meeting on June 28, 1905, chaired by elder Robert Christie, became so "tumultuous that the s was hurried to the front of the church to close the front and keep the sound of the proceedings from reaching the s where a large crowd was gathering." Another report obs that women "stood on the pews waving their handkerchi emotional distress.

Hardly anyone emerged unscathed; tensions perc for at least three years. At one point in 1905, after app in court on complaints (dismissed) from women who s annoyed them, Mr. Denham resigned, moved to Florida t oranges, only to be reinstated in 1908 by a vote of 75 p of the congregation. In the interim in 1906 Robert Christie, with deacon Francis Applegate and elder Joab Banton charged Elizabeth Grannis with disturbing the church's peace and that if she declined to withdraw that the church should "withdraw from her." An ecclesiastical court, quite unusual for Disciples, made up of three elders from outside of New York, upheld the trustees' decision that she should leave the church, which she resolutely refused to do declaring that she had done nothing wrong except declare "the plain truth." Former pastor, B. B. Tyler, when called back to New York from Philadelphia to testify, stated that instead of being president of the Social Purity League, Mrs. Grannis would better be described as the "president of social nastiness." However, a significant minority continually supported Mrs. Grannis.

In looking back it appears that Elizabeth Grannis was an outspoken social activist who acted on her convictions in ways that today would be encouraged and celebrated, but then offended traditional sensitivities. One incident illustrates: Mrs. Grannis adopted a poor, widowed mother and her eight-year-old black child whom she named Christian League after the National Christian League for the Promotion of Purity. To many church members it was outrageous for Mrs. Grannis to bring the child to church services and allow her to sit next to her in the pew just as she would a Caucasian child. The child was accused of "rolling her eyes, wriggling, and smiling throughout [se]rvice." Mrs. Grannis was requested by some to sit with the [child] on the back pew so that "the southern members would not [take] offense." She refused.

[On] the day of her church trial, April 5, 1906, Elizabeth Grannis [arriv]ed for worship, as usual, with Christian League who, [accor]ding to *The New York Times*, was "wearing a toboggan cap [with] a blue tassel that waved like a clock pendulum every time [she s]hook her head and made faces at the newspaper reporters [asse]mbled in the Sunday School room. But during the service, [whil]e seated by Mrs. Grannis, she scarcely moved an eyeball." At the conclusion of the daylong trial the decision was for the congregation "to separate itself from Mrs. Grannis." She could and would continue to worship there each Sunday regardless of the decision.

Ultimately the loyalties of a majority of church members were not confirmed. Mr. Denham was observed traveling through Canada with a young married woman, Emma K. (Mrs. Bartol) Hall, whom he introduced as either his wife or sister. He was named co-respondent in the divorce case of her husband against her. Although numerous other charges were made against Mr. Denham, one conviction by the courts of New York State as reported in *The Christian Evangelist* of October 15, 1908, confirmed Mrs. Grannis's and others' accusations against him.

In spite of the newspaper reports concerning the case of B. Q. Denham, formerly of New

42

York City, but now of Pleasant Hill, Mo., we have declined to make any statement of the case until the trial of the divorce case in which he was co-respondent had taken place. Now that the case has been tried, and he has been pronounced guilty of leading a young wife astray, and bringing about a divorce between herself and her husband, she herself confessing her crime, there remains nothing for us to do but to publish this regrettable fact, that the brethren and churches may act accordingly. We have a note from Brother Denham, together with a statement, denying the charge against him, and saying that he could not defend himself against a wealthy plaintiff. But we cannot go behind the decision of the judge on the testimony offered and the confession of the wife. The case is an awful warning to all ministers of the gospel to guard their conduct in this and all other respects that they may not bring into disrepute the holy cause they represent.

If the editor's accusing the young woman of felonious behavior appears unduly harsh today, it reflects the fact that in most states adultery was still a criminal charge. The turmoil for a time left the congregation dispirited and with a loss of members that new leadership worked to heal.

Elizabeth Grannis continued her attendance at services. While she could be strident in her zeal for justice and moral integrity, the confirmation of her accusations and changing times slowly brought the congregation to a new appreciation of her remarkable contributions. She was one of the pioneering advocates of progressive principles which would soon become fundamental to the congregation. Since her Connecticut childhood she had been a crusader. Denied her request at age

:ach Sunday School because of her youth, she started
/ nurturing an impoverished young child she found
ox in which she had placed a shabby doll, and also
)oor children she found in a haystack. From 1887
1ually re-elected national president of The Christian
the Preservation of Purity.

ited two periodicals. *Church Union,* nationally
for 23 years, was a justice-oriented magazine
breaking down sectarian walls that angered many
.... clergymen. For her editorials she was honored for
her support of the ecumenical cause by the Federal Council of
Churches, which hailed her as occupying "a rightful place among
the strong, forceful women who have given splendid leadership
in the last half century in Christian work and philanthropic
reforms." Her concern for children led her to edit another
magazine, *The Children's Friend and Kindergarten.*

She spoke out in support of the right of women to preside at
the Communion table. For 20 years prior to women achieving
the vote she would annually seek to register as a "female man"
asserting that the Bible stated that God "created man, male
and female he created them." She spoke and wrote against the
sale of tobacco to minors, capital punishment, and corporal
punishment of students. She was a strong supporter and friend
of President Garfield (a member of the Disciples of Christ),
the poet William Cullen Bryant, and the civil rights advocate
Booker T. Washington, all of whom wrote appreciatively of her
contributions. Largely because of her actions the congregation
can claim to have been interracial for more than a century. *The
New York Times* obituary for Elizabeth Grannis at her death
at age 85 in 1926 celebrated this remarkable church member
as "humanitarian, editor, reformer, pioneer suffragette," who
"never stopped trying to make the world a better place according
to her lights."

Two Remarkable Developments

1. The Chinese Sunday School

In 1899, and parallel to the beginnings of the ministry of B. Q. Denham, an impressive development in the congregation's history was making exciting strides. In June 1884, *The New York Times* reported the formation of a Chinese Sunday School Union. For a number of years the Chinese population in New York had been increasing, fueled by the descendants of the Chinese workers who had toiled to build the transcontinental railroad decades earlier, as well as other, often impoverished, immigrants from China searching for new lives. Educational opportunities were all but non-existent. Church folks, observing the need and seeing an evangelistic opportunity, soon were organizing Sunday Schools to teach English, primarily to the boys. Robert Bassett, secretary of the Union said, "That in a practical way [these schools would] found a home in New York where Chinese boys may meet together for social pleasures and mental instruction, and where they may live, if necessary, and grow up to teach their people the ways of Christianity." It was asserted that the schools would provide the young Chinese "greater safety from persecution," a national tragedy for which there were no protective laws.

In the ensuing years scores of Chinese Sunday Schools were founded in New York, Brooklyn, in the surrounding areas of New Jersey, and as far away as Boston. One of the largest, most successful and long-lasting schools began in the early 1890s. It was formally organized by Central Church of the Disciples in September 1899, and continued until 1948.

Its beginnings can be traced back to a Chinese family represented by Chin Fong who owned a laundry near Carnegie Hall and an American photographer and evangelical Christian, Joseph M. Appleton. Chin Fong was the laundryman for the Appleton family. The friendship of these two families combined with Chin Fong's commitment to his children's education and Joseph Appleton's evangelistic concerns opened the way for the next steps. A lady from Central Church came into the laundry and invited the Fong family to the services. Discussions led to the Sunday School which began meeting with four members of the family in attendance. The next week attendance increased to eleven, then fifteen (including the Mook family still active today) and the school was well on its way.

The Chinese were motivated by their hunger for learning and for friendship with Americans. Chin Fong was the interpreter, which was challenging, as he was at first the only one proficient in both languages. Rachel Gleason Brooks, who became a phonetics teacher years later and compiled many of the records of the Sunday School, recalled that "everybody sang and wrestled with the English language." She observed that in the early years almost none of the pupils went to public schools so their entire educational experience was through the Sunday School.

At first the pupils dressed in traditional Chinese clothing, but soon began adopting typical American garb. One tradition, the wearing of the queue (a single long, uncut braided pigtail) was problematic. While the boys longed to cut them short, this would be a capital offense punishable by death if they returned to China. Their solution was to wind the queue around the head and wear a wig over it. Soon the whole school wore wigs. Only after the 1911 revolution which established the Chinese Republic was the law rescinded and they felt free to remove the queue.

By 1904 there were thirty-one students, and because teaching was almost on a one-to-one relationship, eighteen teachers. Evangelistic efforts resulted in many of these boys joining the congregation, and soon two, Chin Yin and Monk Lon, were licensed to preach on the street in Chinatown. In 1906 the Sunday School added YMCA programs of athletics and crafts for the boys. By 1912 attendance averaged fifty. Letters from the families of pupils attest to the overwhelming gratitude for and loyalty to the school.

Another family, that of Len Mook, became involved, and through their efforts a school in Canton, China was established for girls, which by 1917 had a building of its own and forty-five pupils. Increasing missionary and educational efforts in China led to a relationship with the Canton Christian College in Nanking. The pupils and teachers were generous in helping to give financial support to the college and also to Disciples missionary Kate Miller for her work among Chinese women.

For decades church members Mr. and Mrs. James E. Pearce were dedicated superintendents of the New York school. Their appeals for volunteer teachers appeared annually in *Forward*. Christmas was often the setting for a program of readings, recitations, and songs offered by the pupils of the school to the congregation to which the pupils of the sixteen other Chinese Sunday Schools in New York were invited. At one event in 1912 the Chinese and American flags were displayed, and a boy gave a patriotic plea "for a deeper interest in his native land."

One report told of a boy who came to the school, wanted to learn English, but wanted nothing to do with Christianity or any religion. He was, of course, accepted. When the group was assigned to learn the Lord's Prayer, he demurred. The teacher, however, urged him to learn it because it had many English words he would need. In the process of learning he became interested in the Christian faith. Although he never became a church member, when he returned to China he wrote a letter back to the school in gratitude for the school and included that he was working to share the Christian faith with his family and friends. In the course of the school's history at least four Asian Christian congregations were established from the efforts of boys who returned to China

By 1929 more than 100 boys, young men, and teachers were involved in the school, "surely the largest in the city." A *Forward* writer editorialized, "[the school] is one of the most gratifying experiences [in the] history of the church."

The school's reputation brought visitors and fame. The YMCA associated with the school became an integral part of its program. Related Chinese families formed the Disciples "Trust in God" mission in Chinatown in part to give the boys alternatives to gambling. Soon "Trust in God" became the only self-supporting Chinese church in New York. Their influence spread to China where other congregations were organized, and generous benevolent programs were instituted to combat famine and flood relief.

In New York the school continued to serve generations of Chinese youth until 1948. After the close of World War II and the Communist revolution in China, immigration all but ceased and most Chinese were fluent enough in English to attend public school.

Over a half century later the legacy of the Chinese Sunday School has continued to be felt and appreciated in the congregation. Sarah Mook, Martha Butt, and the late Luther Mook, whose families became involved in the church through the school's programs, have actively served in many leadership capacities.

2. Disciples Community House

In the first decade of the 20th century another urban missionary enterprise was born in part through the efforts of Pastor J. L. Darsie. A group of Russian immigrants who shared similar commitments to those of the Disciples of Christ began worshiping and studying English on East Second Street. By 1919 these programs grew into the Disciples Missionary Union devoted to serving foreign groups in the city. Support poured in from other Disciples mission efforts and the Board of Church Extension invested $51,000 in a large town house at 147 Second Avenue at 10th Street which was converted into the Disciples Community House. This was the decade of the height of European immigration which brought vast social upheaval. The lower East Side area of Avenue B, 14th Street, 3rd

48

Street and Third Avenue was the most densely populated area
of its size in the world – 500,000 persons of more than forty
nationalities per square mile. The Disciples Community House
endeavored to answer the overwhelming needs and concerns of
this overcrowded, impoverished community. Daily wages in the
area never exceeded $4.50, more often about $2.00. Programs
were offered to meet almost every possible need: Sunday School;
story hours; kindergarten; English and citizenship classes;
sewing; arts and crafts; dramatics; home visitation; mothers',
boys', girls' and youth clubs; athletics; health clinics; reading
rooms; camping and hiking. In 1920 the number of people
served in one nine-month period totaled 16,000. It was a place
committed to serve the "appalling need of those who otherwise
would be neglected, ... rendering a service in a neighborhood
blessed by its presence, and in the growing assurance that
if Jesus were here, he surely would be found in these human
byways."

The congregation provided volunteers, opened their homes,
and contributed funds for the Community House to send
children to camp every July. Pastor Finis Idleman described
the mission as providing help for "lonely soldiers, newsboys
sleeping on the streets, a home mission as genuine as anything
could be in Tibet or Congo land."

By 1929 the building, always inadequate, became unsafe and
had to be abandoned. Like a second home to the area's children
and families, the mission had grown to serve more than 25,000
annually. Mr. And Mrs. E. M. Bowman of the congregation
and the Woman's Division of the Disciples United Christian
Missionary Society contributed generously to a campaign which
had reached $200,000 in pledges by 1929 to secure a new
home. Sadly, hopes were dashed. The stock market crash and
the subsequent depression made it necessary to abandon the
project.

Ten years later a reunion of the mission was held at Central
Church and 125 returned. Pastor Finis Idleman wrote that their

return was a "testimony that unselfish investment in human life cannot be lost; that when a grain of selfless service falls to the ground it dies and bears much fruit."

From Division and Decline to Healing and Hope

During the emotionally-fraught, difficult time following B. Q. Denham's ministry, a measure of stability was provided by the associate minister from 1901 to 1904, Samuel Guy Inman. Growing up in rural Texas, Inman began his higher education at Texas Christian University. Later, while also pursuing graduate studies at Columbia University, he brought insightful leadership, especially to the Sunday School and the Christian Endeavor program for youth and young adults. He was also instrumental in organizing an orchestra which played for various groups' social programs and attracted new people to the church. While Inman's outstanding contributions to U.S. relationships with Latin America were to be well in the future, his young energy and commitment mitigated recent depressing events.

In 1915 Dr. Inman returned to New York where he and his wife, Bessie Cox, actively participated in the congregation for more than five decades. His outstanding contributions included many publications on U.S/Latin-American relations. He served as delegate to Pan-American and United Nations convocations and as lecturer at Yale and Columbia Universities. In 1956 he initiated Hermosa Center, a "Puerto Rican Cultural Center." He was a leader in the establishment of a Hispanic Disciples congregation in New York, the La Hermosa Christian Church, which today serves at the corner of Fifth Avenue and 110th Street.

The lingering tensions from the Denham debacle brought to

the front a division which had been brewing for decades. The leadership of the congregation was moving inexorably toward a progressive, ecumenical, and biblically liberal approach to the "polar star" of unity so many Disciples sought. However, from ambiguities dating back to the early writings of Alexander Campbell, a significant group was convinced that the only way a true church could be realized was through independently organized congregations recreated on the literal record of the churches described in the New Testament. Already one of the congregation's ministers from decades past, J. Carroll Stark, had debated in favor of instrumental music in worship over against those who opposed it, since no mention is made of instruments in the New Testament documents. A broader and even more contentious issue centered on whether the New Testament permitted a cooperative approach to world missions among denominations or even congregations. Scholarship demonstrating that the biblical record had evolved over centuries deeply disturbed those who were convinced of an inerrant scripture.

The divisions developing among the Disciples of Christ across the nation, especially in the south, inevitably surfaced in the already distressed New York church. During the first decade of the 20th century a small group of dissenters from the congregation began meeting in homes and rented spaces (including an Odd-Fellows Lodge Hall and later at Woods Memorial Chapel on West 69th Street) until 1920, when the Manhattan Church of Christ was organized. Thus, two Christian communities trace their cherished histories back to 1810 and the nine folks meeting in the Ovington home. While many of the issues have not been reconciled in the decades since the division, these two congregations, meeting only a few blocks apart today, work together on behalf of the hungry and homeless and have a positive and filial relationship.

Into the Mainstream

Fortunately, in the midst of these and other tensions help was nearby. Respected Disciples minister Miner Lee Bates was in New York completing a doctoral program at Columbia University in preparation for his appointment as president of Hiram College in Ohio. During this period he had also been serving the sister congregation of Park Avenue Church in East Orange, New Jersey. Persuaded to postpone his work at Hiram for two years (1906-1908), Dr. Bates accepted a pastoral appointment bringing "wisdom and breadth of vision" to the wounded community.

The resulting challenges were many. Budget cuts required the dismissal of the paid quartet, but made possible the development of what would soon become a large volunteer choir, the congregation's first. The immediate area of the church's address on 56th Street was deteriorating. The population from 34th Street to 59th Street on the West Side increasingly consisted of poor Irish immigrants. Gangsters made the area their power base. Called Hell's Kitchen perhaps first by Davy Crockett, the location was making it difficult for the church to attract members, although it was an area in need of mission investment.

Miner Lee Bates was as forward-looking as he was reconciling. He was among the first to point out how Disciples had grown and changed in the nearly 100 years of their history. In an address to the Disciples Convention just after the close of his New York ministry, his plea for unity no longer included a reordering of the church solely on what could be gleaned from the few records of faith communities in the New Testament. He asked if anyone could even imagine publishing a magazine in the 20th century entitled *The Millennial Harbinger,* the major periodical edited by Alexander Campbell. He recognized that Disciples of Christ were evolving into the Protestant mainstream and that the church in New York City should take its rightful place in this tradition. Disciples' rational faith and hope for unity would be based on a spirit of cooperation and covenant which was growing among the various established churches, not on some sort of literal "restoration" of a New Testament era church.

Miner Bates, observing the changing neighborhood, posed a vision (which would be repeated over and over) recommending that the trustees seek a new location to build an enlarged church facility which would serve 1,000 members. He inspired the congregation by his suggestion that the church plan a major centennial celebration in 1910 for its 100th anniversary.

Rose Starratt in her *Sesquicentennial History of the Park Avenue Christian Church* (1960) recalls with appreciation that, at this time, the young poet and artist Vachel Lindsay, while a student at the New York School of Art (later the New School), often joined with church members in the Bates home where "it was a treat to hear – and participate in – his distinctive chanting of his poetry." Lindsay grew up in a very conservative Disciples of Christ, Illinois family and had begun a reluctant education in medicine at Disciples' related Hiram College through which he was introduced to Bates who offered him a more liberal approach to faith. His dedication to art and poetry soon won his full commitment and on moving to New York in 1904 he survived in part by reading and selling his poems and drawings on the street, seeing himself as a modern troubadour. Starratt's memory of Lindsay's "chanting of his poetry" to church members and friends in the Bates home reveals that he was already engaged in developing the style which would lead him to be called "the father of modern *singing poetry*, as he named it, in which verses are meant to be sung or chanted." *Forward* published a poem Lindsay wrote for and presented to the congregation.

> Would that we had the fortunes of Columbus.
> Sailing his caravels, a trackless way,
> He found a universe. He sought Cathay.
> God give such dawns, as when, his venture o'er,
> The sailor looked upon San Salvador.
> God led us past the setting of the sun

To wizard islands, of August surprise.
God makes our blunders wise.

Lindsay's Disciples heritage is honored and remembered today at Hiram College by scholarships awarded in his name.

Dr. Bates's son, Miner Searle Bates, became an outstanding Chinese scholar and faculty member at the University of Nanking until the 1949 Communist revolution. The Bates were invited to New York where he was appointed Professor of Missions at the Union Theological Seminary. He and his wife Liliath were active members, and he served as a respected elder in the congregation from 1950 until his sudden death while hiking at Bear Mountain in 1979. Disciples students at Union Seminary during these years recall the generous Bates hospitality and encouragement with gratitude.

After Miner Lee Bates left for his post at Hiram College, John L. Darsie again served as interim pastor for nine months.

Another fascinating individual was appointed pastor in January of 1909: William L. Fisher, graduate of Bethany College and Yale Divinity School, who also studied at Oxford University and in Germany, Switzerland, and Italy. An outstanding scholar, Fisher had considerable knowledge of Hebrew, Sanskrit, and Greek. Later he served as an honored chaplain of the American 15th Infantry Regiment in China where his explorer's energy is remembered for his personal trek across the vast expanses of the Gobi Desert in 1933.

Also in 1909 the church was finally able to sell their property and move uptown once more. Unable to realize Dr. Bates's vision for a major building program, they nevertheless invested $85,000 in a church building constructed seventeen years earlier by the Third Universalist Society of New York, and had more recently been occupied by the Free Synagogue led by Rabbi Stephen W. Wise. Its Neo-Romanesque sanctuary of Milwaukee brick designed by Jonathan Capen is still located on the Upper West Side at 142 West 81st Street. Between the two square towers are two wide staircases which lead to the sanctuary. At that time the Sunday School, a boys' reading room (girls not allowed?), and library were underneath. The interior was finished in light wood, and the sides were lined with eight stained glass windows. To the right of the Communion Table was a large pipe organ which the church replaced in 1932 with a new 13-rank (1,015 pipes) organ designed by internationally renowned organist Hugh Porter and built by the W. W. Kimball Company of Chicago.

Dr. Porter dedicated the organ in a concert on October 12, 1932, as the congregation celebrated their 122nd anniversary. Here the 280-member congregation embarked on their second century, meeting on West 81st Street until 1945. The church building's walls have echoed to the joyful noises of divergent worship traditions. Since then it has been the home of the Church of Jesus Christ of Latter Day Saints, the Mount Pleasant Baptist Church and school academy, and most recently the Victory Tabernacle Seventh-Day Christian Church.

On October 2 – 9, 1910, the congregation joyfully celebrated their centennial. Former pastors B. B. Tyler and Miner Lee Bates were on hand. H. L. Willett preached and other guests were J. H. Garrison and E. L. Powell, all renowned Disciples leaders of the era. The other Disciples congregations in the area joined in the festivities. For the first time a historical sketch of the congregation's history was compiled by Robert Christie who had begun attending the church as a child in 1851 and had been a member since 1855. It was through his memories and conversations with earliest members that the story of meeting in a Watch House was recalled. Robert Christie died in 1924.

Reconciliation and Progress

W. L. Fisher resigned in 1912 to pursue further studies, and Dr. James McBride Philputt ably served from 1912 to 1916. Well educated at both the University of Indiana and Union

Theological Seminary, he emphasized modern historical biblical scholarship and preached a progressive, liberal, social gospel message. Fully embracing Barton W. Stone's vision of Christian unity as the "polar star" of the Disciples' mission, he became a prominent spokesperson for the emerging ecumenical movement. Dr. Philputt pleaded for the denominations to develop a common missionary alliance and worked at every opportunity for pulpit exchanges and shared congregational experiences. In an address to the Centennial Convention of Disciples in 1910 his remarks on the nature of faith were prescient and a contrast with the "restoration" based calls for unity that had been preached only a few decades earlier.

> Emphasize those things wherein we agree and not those things wherein we differ. Listen to these words from John Ruskin: 'Whenever we allow our minds to dwell upon the points in which we differ from other people, we are wrong and in the devil's power.' That is the essence of the Pharisee's prayer of thanksgiving. 'Lord, I thank thee that I am not as other men are.' At every minute of our lives we should be trying to find out, not in what we differ from other people, but in what we agree.

His vision of Christian unity soared in his final paragraphs:

> A few years ago I stood upon the Isle of Jersey, off the coast of France, where the tide rises twenty feet high. It was low tide and numberless islands were visible here and there. Soon the great tide came rolling in, and one after another these islands disappeared from sight, and when it had reached its height they had all disappeared and I looked out upon an unbroken sea. With the advance of the tide of faith and this knowledge of the Son of God, spirituality will rise higher and

higher. We shall be welded into one great unity and the divisions of to-day will disappear from sight, and be covered as the waters cover the sea. . . . Here [Christian unity], then, is the great purpose of our movement, the thing for which we have stood for a hundred years, for which we shall continue to stand so long as God gives us opportunity.

His vision of the possibilities of Christian unity reflected the mood of the age. An assured New York City and nation were no less optimistic. The Woolworth building and soon others like it scraped the sky. Pennsylvania and Grand Central Stations became the hubs of a national passenger rail system. The decade saw the completion of the Williamsburg and Manhattan Bridges between Manhattan and Brooklyn. This was going to be the American Century, and for Disciples the potential of uniting of the churches would bring Christ to the world.

That spirit inspired another appeal from Dr. Philputt to the next national Disciples convention in Louisville. Although the congregation had recently moved to its new home on 81st Street, he and the church leadership continued to embrace a vision of a Disciples "cathedral" in the nation's metropolis. In an appeal to Disciples everywhere the convention president, E. M. Powell, wrote to Dr. Philputt that it is "impossible to achieve any great things in NY City unless we have a church structure big enough and worthy enough to attract the attention of the thousands of visitors - even our own people - who come to the city. . . . It was my suggestion that this enterprise be made the Centennial monument. . . . I wish our people might see the mighty possibilities of a great institutional church in New York City and they might give the Brotherhood there, all the assistance in the way of money for the doing of a big thing." Dr. Philputt presented the plea to the convention, passed out brochures, and received a positive hearing. On his return to

New York, he expressed that the plea was "launched in a most happy and auspicious manner . . . New York will yet have her innings and our people take their place there as a great, strong religious force in the life of the city and of the nation."

That aspiration would wait four more decades. These early years of the 20th century revealed another story. Underneath and in the shadow of this cornucopia, crime, corruption, and hopeless poverty continued to define millions of the city's people. And in Europe nationalistic competition was darkening the way toward horrific war. The larger church, no less divided regardless of the uniting rhetoric, was immune to none of the underlying tensions.

Primary concerns among the Disciples congregations were directed inward in terms of their own survival and growth. In previous decades the Disciples had sought to increase their presence by establishing other congregations in Manhattan. James Philputt had served two of these prior to being called at First Church — four years at the Disciples congregation on 169th Street and thirteen at the Lenox Avenue Church. His earlier experience in St. Louis in helping unite two congregations into the Union Avenue Church proved invaluable as it became obvious that the Lenox Avenue and the 81st Street congregations would be far more effective if they were to cast their lots together. That Dr. Philputt was well known and respected in both congregations enhanced and helped complete the union. Sixty-four members of the Lenox Avenue congregation joined the First Church at 81st Street on January 14, 1912. The new name of the united congregations: Central Church of Disciples of Christ.

Records show some of the outstanding leaders emerging from the union of the two congregations. Among them are Mr. and Mrs. P. F. Jerome. He, among many accomplishments, received considerable attention as the president of the United States Hay Fever Association and leader of the "New York Hay Fever Club" which had been organized by the famous

Congregational preacher Henry Ward Beecher. Members were said to have tried more than 57 cures for hay-fever and had with tongue-in-cheek sought legislation to outlaw the growth of ragweed in the city's parks. Also remembered are Dr. E. J. Richardson, a respected homeopathic physician with a large practice in St. Luke's Hospital, who with his wife was actively involved. The J. M. Stitt family had been associated with the two congregations since 1899 and Mr. Stitt served into the 1950s as financial officer, president of the board of elders, a life elder, and as director of communion preparation.

Significant growth among youth and young adults was reflected in the active, large Sunday School classes and Christian Endeavor programs. Their evangelistic fervor is revealed in the song they would loudly sing to the tune of "Tipperary."

It's a short way to 81st Street
It's a fine place to go,
It's a short way to 81st Street
To the finest church I know.
Goodbye dear old Broadway,
Farewell Herald Square,
It's a short way to 81st Street
And we'll all be there.

Also during this decade a Young Men's Club was established, a pool table set up, boxing gloves were purchased for the boys, and a baseball team was organized.

Throughout Dr. Philputt's 21 years of ministry in Manhattan, the last four of which were with the Central Church (1912—1916), his progressive zeal for Christian unity was expressed as he and the Manhattan Disciples congregations are listed among the founders and charter members of the New York Federation of Churches which had been established in 1895. The Federation, one of the early ecumenical efforts in the city and the oldest council of churches in the United States, urged the churches to assume greater civic responsibility working toward "municipal progress."

Clearly the congregation had put old issues behind them and was growing not only in membership but also in its mission and ministry. Dr. Philputt increased the reputation of the congregation in the Midwest where the majority of Disciples lived.

Describing his work in New York, Dr. Philputt wrote:

> While church work, especially among our people, is difficult in New York where we are not well known, it still has its compensations. The very fact that we are few in number binds us together and develops a warmth of fellowship known in few other places, and the per capita giving in New York is perhaps greater than in any other church of the brotherhood. While there is much wickedness and corruption in this great city, it is also true that it is the most generous city in the world. . . . Many of the most consecrated Christian leaders are there, and the amount of good done in the city is beyond computation. Such a metropolis cannot be built except by gifted and farseeing leaders who have great ideals and the courage and consecration to realize them. Opportunities for education and culture, for hearing eminent speakers, the finest music, these and many other things help to make a New York pastorate very rewarding.

Among the able student assistants to serve with Dr. Philputt, W. E. Givens is perhaps the best remembered. Later, in 1923, he was appointed director of the boys' division of the Kamehameha Schools in Hawaii, which offered scholarships to students of Hawaiian ancestry. Dr. and Mrs. Philputt visited him on a round-the-world trip to see mission stations.

In tribute to Dr. Philputt, he was invited to preach on the

congregation's 120th anniversary in 1930. Following this service, he related his respect for the congregation and his confidence in his successor, Finis Idleman, in a letter: "I have a profound and growing conviction of the great value of the work this church is now doing. In my sermon, I said the ideal church is yet to be. There is no reason why this church, with its long, noble record, with its splendid nucleus of loyal souls, and especially with the brave and able leadership of Dr. Idleman – there is no reason why Central should not be that ideal church. The broad program and the liberal spirit of the church enables it to minister to a much large community than would be otherwise possible." Regarding his successor, he added, "There is only one Dr. Idleman and no man can fill his place here." Dr. Philputt died in 1932.

Worldly Saints

On January 1, 1916, Finis Idleman came to New York to begin his 25 year ministry, the congregation's longest. Once again, a pastor from a large, thriving Midwestern Disciples congregation – a 3,000 member congregation in Des Moines, Iowa – came to serve a community of fewer than 300 participants in a city where Disciples were all but unknown. Changes over the century since the congregation's founding when New York was overwhelmingly Protestant were emphasized as *The Christian Century* observed that Finis Idleman's "parish" included "more Jews than ever lived in Jerusalem and more Catholics than would be visible to the Pope from the Vatican." His family's story of moving to Manhattan is typical. Transition to close-quartered apartment living for a family with five school-age children was daunting. Public school conditions were not amenable, and needed scholarships for private education were sought and found. A farm in Vermont was offered by E. M. Bowman for retreat and summer holidays.

Pastor Charles E. Jefferson of the Broadway Tabernacle (Congregational) gave the welcoming address dwelling on the significant relationship between the Disciples and the Congregationalists. Within three months after Dr. Idleman's arrival, it was observed by elder Joab H. Banton, District Attorney for the City of New York, that the congregation had "flourished" with growing attendance which "is a wonder . . . . Nothing can withstand the fervor of the heart throb of Finis Idleman. The dormant have awakened, the indifferent become active, the cold fervent." In that three-month period 63 new members were added to the church.

A walking and hiking enthusiast, Finis Idleman, formed a walking club of church members, all of whom fell by the wayside trying to keep his pace. Each summer he climbed Mount Washington by night so as to be at the top for the sunrise. This energetic lifestyle infused his entire ministry. His passionate commitments imbued every task. The famous story of the "iron gates" recalled by James E. Craig, elder, and editorial writer for *The New York Sun*, illustrates.

At that time the portal of the building in West 81st Street was enclosed by two immense grilles which were kept locked on week days. The new minister did not like them; he said that to him they symbolized self-containment and aloofness out of keeping with an all-embracing Christianity. "Our doors should be open to the world," he said. The trustees smiled at his enthusiasm, but said that they knew their New York. Take the grilles down, they argued, and idlers would loiter on the stairways, children would play there, and soon make the place unsightly. "What of it?" asked Dr. Idleman, a question to which there really was no adequate answer. Time went on and this gentle dispute between the minister and the trustees remained unsettled. At last a time came when the pastor was to go away on vacation. His last word before he departed was, "When the gates are down I shall come back." The gates were promptly taken down. . . . Children and idlers . . . have not made themselves nuisances to the church. On the contrary, many youngsters in that congested district found in the Sunday school and daily vacation Bible school a welcome and a warmth of interest in their welfare on the part of Central Church which must surely have brightened their lives. In a very true sense the removal of those barriers symbolized a turning away of the congregation itself from all that had seemed exclusive in the past.

Prophetic in the biblical sense, Finis Idleman constantly challenged the congregation. Following are selections from his *Forward* editorials:

February 1919: "We are rightfully demanding a new church to be worthy of such a mission. It is to be composed of Christians - not church members. We shall know who they are by the 'prints of the nails' of real service. It must be new in its inclusiveness. Denominationalism never looked so mean as now. The church that isolates itself now by any theological or doctrinal barriers will surely be found alone with its unbrotherly spirit ever present as its curse. Likewise the church must forget all past greatness, for the demands to be made now have no precedent."

Following World War I, May 1919. "Two issues seem inevitable for the churches: larger unity and wider knowledge of world conditions. . . . What the war taught is not that God is dead, or indifferent; but only that the task of many is larger, and man's responsibility greater than historic optimism supposed. And if the church is to be the chief instrument for world-redemption, it must cease to esteem its forms and its dogmas, or even itself, as the end of its existence."

February 1922: "Christianity lives by adventure. . . . On this account Christianity must never be permitted to crystallize. When it does it is no longer Christian. Jesus was not a law-giver, he was a life-giver. His kingdom was a passion, not a program. . . . The fear for the church is that it has altogether too much to enjoy and quite too little to endure. . . . We leave every life free in Christ to become its best and highest according to the light which shines in the soul. . . . . Jesus does not limit individuality nor the expression of divergent capacity. . . . *Spiritual freedom [is] central to our church.*"

On ministry in New York City he wrote in April 1923: "New York is not an ideal city in which to do religious work. Always [it is] difficult to maintain a genuinely Christian church in this city where the obstacles are mountain high. Difficulties here are all knotted and multiplied. There are 38 fewer Protestant churches today than in 1898. To build a church in NYC is like a boy building a castle in the sand on the beach when the tide is coming in. New York preachers preach to a procession; people simply vanish. Yet, there is no more glorious place under Heaven in which to proclaim the life and principles of Jesus than just here. What an opportunity to proclaim in the greatest city in the New World the secret of peace and power and gladness!"

Peace-making was central to his faith. In May 1922 he wrote: "The moral equivalents of war are far more effective than fighting if they are trusted to operate. There a hundred steps that could be taken before war is even contemplated. And we know that not one of them was fully tried out before the resort to arms [in World War I]. Vicious journalism is whipping it up with constant threats of the designs of this nation and that against the United States. But other nations have learned their lesson in an even sadder school than ours."

Against the grain of American isolationism, Idleman appealed for U.S. involvement in the World Court, the League of Nations and participation in the Kellogg Peace Pact. As the

Nazis asserted their racist, anti-semitic agenda in Germany, he was among the first to condemn their atrocities. In a 1932 sermon condemning Nazi persecutions, he quoted Helen Keller. "Do not imagine that your barbarities to the Jews are unknown here."

In 1936 as war threats increased, he searched for alternatives. "Only the church in country-wide extent is lifting up its voice in the protest against vast army and navy appropriations; against a forced patriotism which is seeking to militarize the nation into heel-clicking regimentation. . . . Instead of making our country such that one cannot but be proud of it, laws are being passed to compel an artificial patriotism. All this stimulates a false nationalism which is the very atmosphere out of which wars begin. It is just here the church must speak."

The congregation was not unanimous in support of Dr. Idleman's commitments. Yet most were proud that their pastor was black-listed in Elizabeth Dilling's 1935 "Handbook of Radicalism for Patriots – Red Network," in which, because of his prophetic Christianity, he was accused of communist sympathies. Equal to his passion for human rights and social justice was his pastoral and spiritual passion that brought him overwhelming respect and love. The Church accepted his challenge to a more worshipful, spiritual experience. He often appealed to people "to refrain from visiting during morning voluntary [prelude]." He claimed there is "no excuse for very poor reverence for any conversation to be carried on whatsoever, but at the close of the service, when have all gotten the best that the hour could give and have felt that touch of spirit until the benediction, then we may find encouragement and joy in the good fellowship which may reasonably follow." The liturgy and musical offerings of the services became "deeply spiritual experiences." He proclaimed the singing of "the great hymns of the Church Universal. . . . The pietistic and sentimental songs which an era of high pressure evangelism give us are inadequate to liberate and lift the soul. We impoverish our lives by our pitiful self limitation to a few familiar numbers."

Holy Communion — not preaching — was at the very heart of worship. Questioning Alexander Campbell's rationalistic understanding of the Lord's Supper as an ordinance, Idleman embraced its sacramental dimensions, calling the feast, "not so much an obligation as a privilege, not under the law but under grace. . . . Only the hungry of heart can know the secret of His passion."

From 1916 to 1923 the congregation's mission and benevolence giving increased from $2,000 to $16,000. As Wall Street crashed in 1929 and the depression followed, the congregation nevertheless added thousands more to its benevolence contributions. Dr. Idleman observed:

> The church was born in a crisis and ought to be at home in one. The church can minister to human need. Employment must be found for men and women. Food, clothing and shelter must be provided for penniless people, both within and without the church. . . . The spirit of the early Christians must be reproduced when "all things were in common." Those who have, must share with those who have not. . . . The Church must lift its voice for social justice. An economic system that puts 30% of all the wealth of America in the hands of 1% of its people is both indefensible and unchristian. . . . Unemployment, accident and old age security must be secured for every toiler. Capital must regard itself as socially responsible. . . . It is not charity men want but justice and security. The cause of the poor is forever the cause of Christ.

The Idleman pastorate coincided with the height of the temperance movement and the passage of the 18th amendment to the Constitution prohibiting the sale of alcoholic beverages.

Like many Protestant clergy of the time, he was fervent in his
support of prohibition, worked to see its enactment and later
was lonely in his eloquence as he saw defeat coming in 1933:
"Its record is written in blood. No Christian will weaken the
Eighteenth Amendment by vote of personal practice. When the
storm rages, he is traitor who weakens the dikes."

The liberating heritage of the congregation's past was
enhanced, and the progressive approach to faith was fully
established in these decades. Two of Dr. Idleman's editorials
give evidence:

January 1926: "The four fold measure of any church is its
liberty, liberality, loyalty and love. . . . The freedom of thought
which it allows is its own highest compliment. The open
mindedness with which any congregation invites truth from any
source is a tribute to its intelligence."

November 1927: "One of the most beautiful names for a
Christian communion is the one we wear — Disciples. It means
that those who wear it are learners, students of Christ. It implies
that they have open minds and welcome new truth. It would be
incongruous in a disciple to close his mind or to get in a rut. . . .
Intolerance will be as foreign to him as cruelty to a gentleman.
The idea of excluding any one who possess the spirit of Christ
is impossible. Because he is forever learning he believes that
others have truth which he should know and grace he should
imitate."

His ecumenical zeal accompanied his liberal commitments.
Encouraging the emerging unity conversations between the
Congregationalists and Disciples, he reminded his congregation
that it was time for Disciples to accept persons from other
baptismal traditions. In February 1922 he wrote that it is a
"grievous sin to subscribe to the policy of receiving only the
immersed" into church membership, a prophetic stance that
led the New York congregation to the forefront and influenced
many Disciples congregations to adopt an "open membership"
position in future years. As an early chairperson of the Disciples

Council on Christian Unity, Idleman pioneered in developing a long and fruitful relationship of the congregation with ecumenical institutions, including the Federal and National Council of Churches and the Consultation on Christian Union.

In the midst of a challenging public ministry Finis Idleman embraced a cherished family life. A remarkable essay from Finis Idleman's granddaughter, Margaret Stearns Burdett, remembers delightful times visiting her Grandpa. From the age of four she occasionally spent the summer with Grandpa and Grandma Idleman and their five children at the Springfield, Vermont retreat provided by the congregation's Bowman family. Life there included two-day drives in an open roadster punctuated by numerous flat tires. She recalls that, fortunately, there was little traffic in those days and Dr. Idleman's erratic driving never led to difficulties. This was a working farm with a large apple orchard, and the boys, Harold, Holland, and Hillis, were expected to do farm chores dressed in starched, white shirts, which their mother, May, and sisters, Margaret and Miriam, were expected to keep clean, even while they produced three hardy meals a day. She recalls that "Grandpa's great joy was the cabin on a nearby hillside to which he would retire each morning to work on correspondence and to plan his sermons for the coming year." Despite his weak heart, he had unbounded enthusiasm. She wrote, "I remember in particular the day that he discovered a dead chicken in the barnyard, cut it open, and couldn't wait to show me where eggs come from. I'm afraid that my response wasn't gratifying." At home in nature, Finis Idleman tended a vegetable garden, grew beautiful raspberries and built a stone fireplace for cookouts by the lake.

Later on she recalls exciting expeditions to visit her grandparents at their New York apartment on Riverside Drive. Trips to Central Church included the attractions of a jar of hard candy on her Grandpa's desk and the exotic sounds of recitations by the children in the Chinese school. Best of all were trips to the Bronx Zoo that resulted in her Grandpa sending her "doggerel poems about the animals we had seen."

As active, involved, and articulate as Finis Idleman was, the congregation matched him. These were years of a multi-class Sunday School, fellowship and service groups, and outstanding lay and student intern leadership. The dedicated women's organization transformed itself into a branch of the Red Cross during the first World War. While sewing thousands of surgical dressings and bandages to be shipped overseas, they also found time to entertain and feed hundreds of soldiers and sailors, often wounded, as they disembarked in New York on returning from France. After the war they continued their work, sewing clothing, underwear, and hospital shirts by the thousands for the refugees left by the conflict. In the late 1930s, they returned to these tasks, plus knitting sweaters to help support those who were resisting the Nazi and fascist regimes.

Many young adult activities centered around the Sunday Evening Club which sponsored a cornucopia of activities including dances with live orchestras (one intriguingly called The Dixie Jubilee Swingers), weekend trips, picnics, annual talent programs, and, with the Christian Endeavor group, an annual Halloween party complete with "spooks, black cats, witches, chamber of horrors, ghost stories and all the accessories." Dramatic presentations included "After Wimpole Street" a sequel to the "Barretts of Wimple Street," and at Christmas, "While Mortals Sleep," among many others. Sports now included a basketball as well as baseball team. Each fall the Idlemans hosted a breakfast for scores of Disciples-related college students from out of town enrolled in the city's universities.

Service and educational projects were not neglected. The Sunday Evening Club sponsored speakers on the nature of war and peace and reconstruction efforts following the Armistice. The group joined with the women in support of the recently established Disciples Mission House on Second Avenue, especially the Bertha Merrill Girls Club where the participants were quoted pleading, "We want to learn. Teach us something." Children and youth activities were no less dynamic. Large Sunday School classes with names such as "Loyal Workers," "The Twentieth Century Limited," and "The True Blues" competed for attendance records. These were augmented by Boy and Girl Scout troops. A boys' choir was organized. Free all day excursions for neighborhood children to upstate Bear Mountain were provided annually at church expense. In November 1923 *Forward* reported:

> A distinguished guest stepped in to Central Church not long ago on a week day and saw troops of children coming in from their play on the streets. When he learned that this was a service the church was rendering to the community and that all of the children belonged to Jewish and Catholic families or to non-religious homes, he was astonished at the unselfishness of such an exciting program. As a business man he remarked that few people knew what the church was doing to build a nobler citizenship and to create a better world.

Community and national issues were addressed by a variety of guest speakers including theologians Reinhold Niebuhr, Paul Scherer, as well as by Samuel Guy Inman on his worldwide efforts for peace, especially in Latin America.

Long time congregational leader, Robert Christie, was honored as the first person to receive the recognition as "Fellow in Perpetuity" of the (Disciples) United Christian Missionary Society for his gift of $10,000. Another, Lloyd Maxwell, was appointed to head a committee to work toward a new church building. Plans were drawn; funds were made available for preliminaries. Building Fund pledges were urged. The vision of a great Disciples center in New York was a steadfast but elusive dream in these years.

That the congregation remained so committed is a testament to the nature of its people and pastors. Dr. Idleman summarized his evaluation of their mission in comments made to new members in 1933:

> Now you have come to New York. Not in all your life have you seen so much need and so few to meet it. Never has any experience of yours seen the church work under such difficult conditions or against so many hindrances as in this city. . . . For 120 years this church has kept its candle burning in this metropolis. More than four generations of families have shared its 'rock in a weary land, its covert in the time of storm.' Many more generations of transient participants have found here their refuge and their inspiration. While hundreds of churches have been blotted out in this [city's] maelstrom, this self-sacrificing fellowship has possessed a vitality that continues undimmed its ministry of the spirit of Christ to the vast human needs of a great city. We have entered into a noble inheritance. . . . Because many loved the church more than their own comforts or their personal opinions or even their lives we have this spiritual home today. Only as we love it equally and wisely well can we perpetuate it to those who are to follow us.

That spirit prevailed. Music ministries were significantly enhanced by the coming of Solon Alberti as organist and director of choirs. He became a permanent resident of New York City after the rising evil in Nazi Germany had made it impossible for him, a Jew, to accept a position as a conductor at the Munich Opera House.

He would often remark that the opportunity to serve the church and offer sacred music was a "major turning point in my life." In his first year, 1931, a four decade series of major choral concerts was inaugurated with J. S. Bach's "St. Matthew Passion." The choir grew in size and ability, attested to by their many concerts and invitations to sing on the radio. In April 1933, more than 600 were in the audience for Mendelssohn's "Elijah," presented in dramatic form. *Forward* called the program a "landmark in the history of Central Church." A two record album of "The Christmas Story" told in anthems sung by the choir with narration by Ira Langston was released commercially and sold nationally in 1950. In 1955 the choir performed on national television on Easter morning. A decade later another performance of "Elijah" in 1964 was so successful that the choir was invited to perform it at the Temple of Religion at the New York World's Fair. Until Solon Alberti's retirement in the 1970s, the choir presented many of the Romantic era's oratorio repertoire in concerts each season. An honored and beloved staff member, he said he stayed "because I always felt at home here," a testimony by no means unusual.

Finis Idleman's ministry continued to expand in significant ways. His ecumenical commitment was expressed as he served as chairperson of the organization that would become the Council on Christian Unity. His admiration for and friendship with Peter Ainslie III, "a towering figure among 20th century ecumenists," led him in 1941 to write, *Peter Ainslie, Ambassador of Good Will*, a major biography. Idleman shared with Ainslie in rejecting the "power of denominational idolatry" and in emphasizing openness for all Christians regarding church membership and in the celebration of Holy Communion.

An outpouring of gratitude and praise for his ministry followed Finis Idleman's unexpected death in March 1941. Audrey Platnick and Sarah Mook, two who have served as elders and today remember him, affirm that his prophetic utterances by this time had become legendary. His final editorial in *Forward* written a day before his death was prescient.

What makes a church? . . . Why it is a part of

that eternal procession we hear singing as they pass, and as they go just beyond us and out of our hearing. I heard them last Sunday. The church I love was among them. How proudly I turned my head on my pillow to see if they were not coming in. But the tide of the church moved on. That is its way. Who was I that I could divert it? But it was enough that I knew it was a part of that grand procession; that its men and women, boys and girls were on their quest of that Holy Grail. It was enough. In the chamber of my isolation I could now wait until my release for I had seen the triumph from afar. The church I serve did not depend on me. It had caught the vision from afar. The Pilgrim's Chorus was on its lips and the break of Easter morning was in its eyes. There is an everlasting something about the church. It lives on despite poverty and death; despite persecution and calamity.

Writer and elder James E. Craig celebrated his life in the next *Forward* on March 27:

Central Church has been unusually fortunate in having had for more than twenty-five years a veritable prophet for its pastor... [Finis Idleman] taught us that true Christianity is not a web of dogma and doctrine, but a way of life. . . . Almost every text he ever used for a sermon was some word spoken by the Savior. . . . [His credo was] 'Where Jesus speaks, I speak, and concerning the needs of the human soul, Jesus is never silent.'... Though he was a man of strong convictions, his way of winning others to them was always a way of love and gentleness – a triumphant way as in the end, it always proved. His love of beauty was so great and intense that he could not do or say unbeautiful things. . . . In a very real sense he was a martyr to every cause he believed in. . . . We of Central Church are the inheritors of graciousness, of tolerance, of kindliness, of sacrifice, of high and mystic idealism, and above all, of a faith that is as serene and deep and strong as a mighty river.

Impetus for Change:
Post-war Recovery and New Hopes

With the sudden death of Finis Idleman, assistant pastor Ira W. Langston was thrust into pastoral leadership. James E. Craig recalled this period three years later at the congregation's 135th anniversary celebration: "The death of this able and saintly pastor, plunged Central Church into another era. Many close friends and devoted members of the church feared that his death was the beginning of the end for the church they all loved."

Fortunately Ira W. Langston had come to New York to study at Union Seminary that year and was working with Dr. Idleman as the student assistant. Into this bleak and empty house of despair stepped this young man with a message of comfort and courage. It is still difficult to be sure exactly how he came to be called to the pastorate. He was only 28 years of age. He made no application nor did any group organize a movement for the purpose of electing him. Perhaps it was a move of desperation, or perhaps it was just meant to be. Be that as it may, in June of 1941, the congregation unanimously accepted the recommendation that Ira W. Langston be called as successor to Dr. Finis S. Idleman.

To Ira Langston's credit, the ministry, mission, and programs of the church continued and strengthened in the years that followed. Light was beginning to penetrate the darkness of war. The people were united in support of the efforts toward victory. The congregation, especially through the leadership of the women, continued to be involved in helping with the "magnitude" of need for clothing for "the extremely needy in the liberated countries of Europe." The Women's Council baled and shipped thousands of items. *Forward* cautioned that "formal dresses are not needed."

One of the major undertakings following victory was to provide support for Congressional passage of legislation that would permit the entry into the United States of a much larger share of displaced persons who were existing in United Nations sponsored recovery camps in Germany, Austria, and Italy. Clara Roe, chair of the church's committee on Human Relations, reported that of the more than one million displaced persons in these camps, 200,000 were Jewish, a third of the remainder were Protestant or Orthodox Christians, and that "some of these are relatives of members of our own church."

The war, however, didn't dampen the great vision of the past decade shared by the pastors and church members, which so strongly motivated their new minister – to find a suitable new home for the congregation so that the "church could enhance and fulfill its just and responsible role in the affairs of the city."

The Quest for a New Home

Beginning in May 1944, the congregation tingled from the reports in every issue of *Forward* of the possibility of acquiring a new, enlarged church facility on the East Side. Ira Langston with real estate agent and church member Isabel Cleaver, had discovered the opportunity to purchase an empty, architecturally outstanding church building on the corner of "silk-stockinged" Park Avenue and 85th Street. When the idea was presented to the congregation, *Forward* reported that "the spirit of the group was enthusiastic, eager, and united in the hope that something might be worked out." The building was opened for inspection by all interested and the trustees were empowered to begin negotiations with the Brick Presbyterian Church Corporation, which, with the Presbytery of New York, were the owners of the building. Knowing that the congregation would not, on its own, be able to purchase the building, discussions with Disciples national organizations were begun to enlist support for the project from across the nation. By September the congregation had pledged nearly $50,000. With the help of contributions from the Disciples mission cooperative, the United Christian Missionary Society, and mortgage funds from the Board of Church Extension, the people unanimously authorized $200,000 to purchase the building, to be paid over three years. With negotiations concluded in late 1944, the move to the new building occurred, quite appropriately, on Valentine's Day, 1945.

Meril May, chair of the committee on expansion, concluded that a "wonderful dream" and a "staggering undertaking" had overcome "one obstacle after another" and the congregation stood "on the threshold of one of the greatest opportunities that has ever been offered to a small group of Christian people." Lloyd Maxwell, chair of elders, brought the challenge into focus.

> It is not enough to say we are moving to Park Avenue. Owing to that move, our obligation has increased many fold. Look back upon our quiescent, easy going Central Church of a year ago, and you may well claim that we are now almost supermen and superwomen. Then we were blind, now we see. Then we were broke, now we are to occupy a million dollar church. Then we were resting in a chrysalis, now we have bursted [sic] the shell and are out in the world attempting to fly.

Had the nation not been at war, the purchase would likely have been thwarted. The land alone on Park Avenue was so valuable that real estate interests pursued purchasing the church edifice, demolishing it, and erecting another of the buildings that have created the upscale canyon of high-rise apartments from midtown to 96th Street. Preservation interests were feeble to non-existent in those days, and only the inability to obtain building materials in wartime stopped the sale. So easily and quickly this wondrous sacred space could have disappeared, as did many architectural gems until the 1963 demolition of the magnificent Pennsylvania Station finally became the catalyst for the enactment of the city's first architectural preservation statutes.

What did the congregation get? More than they dreamed. In addition to finding a home in a landmark edifice that the *The New York Times* called "one of the handsomest churches in the city," the location helped make possible their survival in the difficult years ahead when scores of other historic churches in the city would languish and close. The church building is almost completely the work of architect Bertram Goodhue of the firm Cram, Goodhue and Ferguson, who is noted for his commitment to Neo-Gothic architecture. Inspired by the royal chapel the Sainte-Chapelle in Paris, the church is built in the ancient tradition of buttressed stone with no steel support, making it far more authentic than most Gothic-style buildings of the 20th century. From its soaring *fleche* (tower) to its impressive interior arches of ribbed vaulting, handcrafted oak carvings, and lofty windows — including three of magnificent stained glass by Louis Comfort Tiffany – it fully deserves the designation as a "Landmark of New York" given by the New York Community Trust.

The story of this building since its 1909 beginnings is instructive. Old South (Dutch Reformed) Church (officially the Reformed Protestant Church of Garden Street, named for its previous location near City Hall) which erected the building, was likely the oldest continuing congregation in New York, having been founded in the old Dutch fort during the early settlement of *Niew Amsterdam* on Manhattan Island in the 1630s. In 1909, the congregation, then located on Madison Avenue and 38th Street, decided to abandon their stone church in the Murray Hill district and seek a location further uptown. At first they purchased lots at Park Avenue and 83rd Street, the same space that our Central Church had considered but abandoned earlier as too far uptown. However, the site was deemed too small for the congregation's plans. A livery stable vocally opposed by the neighbors had begun construction on a larger tract on the southeast corner of 85th Street and Park Avenue. A trade was possible. Over $1,000,000 was involved in the transaction. The cornerstone was soon laid, and the transcendent building was dedicated in 1912.

Real estate contingencies intervened. Entrepreneur philanthropist, August Hecksher, had offered to purchase Old South Church's Madison Avenue property for enough funds to cover the costs of their new building plus providing the church with a $200,000 endowment. However, legal challenges regarding zoning restrictions in the Murray Hill district made it impossible for him to complete his building plans, and the sale was abandoned. Without these funds and having no prospect for selling their property for its previously assumed worth, Old South Church within three years sadly could not pay their creditors, disbanded as a congregation, and the property was sold.

In 1914 the building became the new home of the Union Presbyterian Church renamed the Park Avenue Presbyterian Church. It had few changes when the congregation merged in 1940 with the newly-erected Brick Presbyterian Church at Park Avenue and 91st Street. The building remained essentially unused except for a small Finnish Lutheran congregation that continued to meet there for services after Central Church purchased it in 1944. While touring the facility prior to its purchase, Central

Church members remember observing homeless persons living in and "protecting" the abandoned building. That deplorable tradition of neglecting the poor continues. The Park Avenue church steps as well as those of many other houses of worship are still home to the packing case "tents" of the homeless in search of a secure place to sleep.

Assertive Leadership

The ministry of Ira W. Langston continued until 1954. An assertive preacher, he was an outspoken proponent of progressive Protestantism, religious liberty, and ecumenism. He participated in a debate on NBC radio regarding the existence of God. A Protestant Communion Service was televised for the first time in 1952 by NBC from Park Avenue Church, sponsored by the Radio and Film Department of the National Council of Churches of Christ in America. Ira Langston used his flair for the dramatic to make his points. He could be a strident preacher, declaring that New York City had "sunk deeply into the muck of moral degradation, like Sodom, rotten to the core." On Christmas Eve in 1953, he confessed that he was the "refugee from a madhouse" who introduced a discordant symbol into (the church's) Christmas reveries, and placed "an offering box before the cross" among the poinsettias on the Communion Table. His reason: the congregation's "self-deception." He wrote that "our congregation is in no position to sit back demanding unfettered beauty and perfect harmony," when "we are out of balance ourselves." Declaring that "the mortgage is due and God has no funds except what we give," the pastor demanded that $12,000 in "new and unexpected money" be provided before the end of the year. Apparently funding arrived, since the mortgage payments were made.

Throughout the congregation's history, informed, able leadership in liberal causes has been provided from among the church membership. In the mid-20th century this was especially true. Samuel Guy Inman, a life elder, was often absent because of his international commitments in Asia, Europe, and especially in South America. In the early days of the continuing crisis between Israel and Palestine, Dr. Inman was a member of the American Christian Palestine Committee, responding to the United Nation's internationalization of Jerusalem. He was a frequent speaker in the United States and Europe in the interest of world peace. Respect for his leadership of the inter-denominational forces for Latin American missions brought him three "nicknames" from the congregation: "Sunshine Guy Inman, Steam-engine Guy Inman, and Spiritual Guy Inman." "Great throngs" of students at Columbia University would "flock" to his Sunday morning Young Men's Class at the church.

Emory and Myrta Ross were deeply involved in issues on the African continent. As a member of the African Committee of the Foreign Missionary Conference, Dr. Ross lectured frequently, and one of his most significant contributions was his address to the Menninger Clinic in Topeka, Kansas, on "The Effects of Western Civilization on Primitive Peoples." Myrta Ross offered untiring leadership and nurture to the congregation on the church's mission in response to the needs of the African population. She was recognized internationally for her contributions and spoke to Protestant groups in Italy, France and Germany.

Meril May served the congregation in almost every office. As vice-president of the National Layman's Advisory Commission, he was cited for his impact on behalf of the congregation across the nation.

Along with his position as opinion editor of *The New York Sun*, James E. Craig, was selected to edit *The Protestant World*, a nationwide Protestant newspaper in 1950. A church member of whom it was written that "his knowledge of the Christian religion is exceeded only by his devotion to Jesus Christ," Craig served both as president of the board of trustees and as elder.

W. Earl Waldrop, associate pastor from 1948 through 1950, was influential in reorganizing the congregation in a more functional manner, founding a men's club, a young married's group, a junior high Chi Rho fellowship, and helping establish a nursery school in the church. Called "brilliant" in his guidance of the Sunday Evening Club of young adults, he was energetic in his contribution to the overall ministry of the church. From this post he was called to the large, prominent Central Christian Church in San Antonio, Texas, where he also served with distinction.

Positive changes in Protestant-Catholic relations, which would bear fruit after the 1960 Vatican Council, were strained only eight years earlier. When President Harry Truman proposed establishment of diplomatic relations with the Vatican in 1952, the Park Avenue congregation fully embraced the substantial Protestant opposition. Samuel Guy Inman wrote long essays emphasizing that such a move would exalt the political prestige of a church that was opposed to the voluntary nature of American religious experience. He related that the rejection of the Roman Catholic hierarchy in Mexico was essential to that nation's revolution and independence. He wrote, "Such an act would mean the immediate downfall of a Mexican government, if not an armed revolution." James E. Craig weighed in with a less polemical statement urging members to make their decision "on their knees in the closet of prayer." While appreciating the sacred history and contributions of the Catholic Church, numerous *Forward* articles strongly urged members to write to the President and Congress regarding their position on establishing diplomatic relationships with the Vatican. The proposal was defeated at that time. Attitudes subsequently changed, and three decades later few Protestants opposed the 1984 decision of Congress to approve this recognition.

Suddenly in January 1954, Ira Langston abruptly resigned in the midst of a worship service and walked out of the sanctuary. The tactical reason was for the same purpose as his earlier placement of an offering box on the Communion Table among the poinsettias at Christmas: to wake up a congregation he felt was not meeting its obligations and potential. A committee was appointed by Holland B. Idleman, son of Finis Idleman and chair of the Official Board, to seek a minister and to give prior consideration to recalling Mr. Langston. However, his impulsive resignation was accepted "with deep regret of our minister for thirteen years," and afterwards he was called to the presidency of Eureka College, a Disciples institution in Illinois. In the interim Jack Forstman, Union Seminary graduate student and associate in ministry who later became the dean of Vanderbilt Divinity School, was the fortunate choice for preacher.

A Decisive Decade

In May 1954, providence once again smiled on the congregation. Hampton Adams, M.A., B.D. (Yale University and Divinity School), D.D. (Transylvania University), who for sixteen years was the pastor of the large, urban Union Avenue Christian Church of St. Louis, Missouri, accepted Park Avenue Church's call. *Forward* carried this comment: "Surely the hand of God has been moving in our midst! Where but from On High could we have received the courage, the vision and the enthusiasm to be so bold as to extend a call to the distinguished minister of a church five times the size of ours? What but an assurance of God's bidding could have led this minister, who has declined calls to great churches, to teaching positions and to places of leadership in seminaries and other Brotherhood [denominational] institutions to accept the call of the Park Avenue Church?" The St. Louis congregation responded by calling Dr. Adams "the outstanding statesman of the brotherhood. While the Park Avenue church is not among our largest congregations, its strategic importance calls for a man of Dr. Adams' qualifications. He leaves one great church and ministry to go to another. . . ."

On the 144th anniversary of the congregation, October 10, 1954, ten outstanding religious organizations of the nation joined the congregation in installing Hampton Adams as minister. He was joined by his wife, Adelaide, who soon became beloved for her pastoral qualities combined with her musical contributions and the beautiful hats for which she was justly famous. They had two sons, John P. and Harry Baker Adams, and a daughter, Ruth (Mrs. Ruth Graham). Harry Baker Adams was also called to ministry and served for many years on the faculty of Yale Divinity School.

During the first weeks of his ministry positive interfaith relationships were subtly launched from the bulletin board outside the building. Max Borgenicht, a member of the Park Avenue Synagogue, wrote: "I reside in the neighborhood of your church and was much impressed the other day when I noticed on the bulletin board your greetings to the Jewish people on the Jewish New Year. I would like you to know that your good will gesture did not go unnoticed and was favorably commented on by a good many of my friends who live in the neighborhood. I wish that such gestures could be multiplied throughout the world."

In less than a year Dr. Adams succeeded in another neighborhood benefit. Provocatively named gangs of teenage boys were all but synonymous with New York neighborhoods in the 1950s. The Sharks and Jets of "West Side Story" had their counterparts in the East Side's Hell Benders and Dukes. A two-column feature in The New York Times which pictured Hampton Adams described how he learned from the police that these two gangs operated in the shadow of the church and that an opportunity to change their direction was possible. The leader of one had joined the Navy and the other was in jail. Dr. Adams challenged the church to provide leadership for the masses of boys who were using the streets and sidewalks for "recreation and mischief." In a sermon entitled "The University of the Home" he declared, "We are the church and are responsible not only for making our own homes Christian, but also for giving leadership and aid to those people whose home life is depressed, especially children and youths. . . . If we do not do this, the guilt for juvenile delinquency in Yorkville can be laid at our doorsteps." With congregational support, meeting space for the gangs was provided in the church building, and the YMCA contributed professional recreation leaders for the boys.

Serving on major national boards and holding high ecumenical and Disciples offices, Hampton Adams was at the center of liberal Protestantism. He served as a delegate to the World Council of Churches meeting in Evanston, Illinois in 1954, and the same year was elected to the board of Union Theological Seminary. Among his books is a theological primer, *A Vocabulary of Faith*, and one of a series on various denominations, *Why I am a Disciple of Christ*. His zeal for Christian unity led him to declare that all "Protestantism should be embarrassed and compromised by the divisions among us, but let us not underestimate the unity of the church." Periodically he would teach the Polity Class for Disciples seminarians at Union Seminary where many of his students learned to embrace the whole church from his understanding of the Lord's Supper (for him: "Holy Communion") and baptism as not simply New Testament ordinances, but as sacramental acts in which God's presence is to be experienced and celebrated. On social issues, as well, he did not shy away from controversy, declaring that "birth control is the right of all Christians."

During the late 1950s a major mission opportunity presented itself to the congregation when Dr. Larimer and Gwen Mellon, impressed by the congregation's openness and diversity, were baptized and became members. Dr. Mellon, heir to the Andrew Mellon fortune and impressed by the work of Albert Schweitzer in Africa, was inspired to devote his life, as well as his personal wealth, to develop a desperately needed medical mission. As a result the Mellons founded and directed the Albert Schweitzer Hospital near Deschapelles, Haiti, which provided free medical care to the people of that area who otherwise had no access to health services. Park Avenue Church elder, the Rev. Dr. Emory Ross, was the principal speaker at the hospital's dedication. While the Mellons were rarely able to be present in worship, the church's support for their mission was ardent. Mission offerings were regularly sent. The hospital was a primary service project of the Christian Women's Fellowship for decades. In 1963 a school, Ecole la Providence, was added to provide high academic nurture and sound Christian ethics. The hospital grew to 160 beds with a medical staff of 14 who treated over 500 outpatients annually. Norman Cousins, editor of *The Saturday Review*, in an extensive report about their work, concluded that "Larimer Mellon, like Albert Schweitzer, is in the business of creating a new image for the white man. In an age of blistering color consciousness, this comes close to being the most important business in the world."

An Exuberant Era

The congregation established some of its most ambitious programs and projects in the 1950s. At Dr. Adams's suggestion the numerous talented actors in the congregation founded what would become one of the oldest, successful Off Off Broadway theaters in New York, the Ten Ten Players. "Mother founder" Leslie Bidwell, with the help of Wayne Umphlett and Sybil Lavengood, launched the group in 1955 on a stage built by the church's YMCA Boys' Club. Some of its most successful productions were staged in the chancel of the sanctuary, including a stunning production of the medieval drama "Everyman" in 1959. Through more than five decades hundreds of amateur and professional actors and technicians have offered well-received dramas, comedies, musicals and children's theater productions. Participants have always included persons from the community, as well as church members. Among the early talented and committed stalwarts of the theater and congregation were June Glover, Bill Calhoun, Wayne Umphlett, and one who served in many capacities as deacon, elder, and choir member, Carmon "Cap" Caplinger.

Throughout the 20th century, and beyond, young adult couples and singles fellowship/study groups flourished and made significant contributions to congregational life. Waxing and waning with various names, the Gothamites, Sunday Evening Club, Twenty-niners, the Book Review Group, and Wednesday Evening Christian Fellowship usually met in members' homes. Jo Ann Ashley recalls the many gourmet dinners, cake decorating birthday celebrations, creating individual plaster "death" masks, and "levitations," a parlor game where a person seated in a chair was lifted into the air. A number of romances flourished into marriage out of the group including that of British immigrant Walter Ashley to Jo Ann. Walter discovered the group in a pamphlet, "Things for Singles to do in New York." The most recent incarnation with a more sociological identification is called the "XY Group."

While the congregation possessed "one of the most magnificent church edifices in New York City," the parish facilities were not only inadequate but unsafe. The Fire Department warned the church of the dangers of holding a church school in a building with a wooden stairway. Early in Hampton Adams's ministry ambitious plans began to emerge for a "mighty beginning" of a new parish facility. In 1959 an anonymous gift of $100,000 toward the building and another gift for engineering and architectural studies were catalysts. The congregation, searching for a way to serve their immediate community with a new facility, consulted the nearby Lenox Hill Neighborhood Association. Their survey indicated that the most pressing need was for early childhood education. As a result a major portion of the new building would include a day school specifically designed for children ages 3 through 5. In addition, since the congregation was often host to missionaries traveling overseas, it was hoped that accommodations for temporary hospitality could also be included. A large fellowship hall would serve many functions including a stage constructed for the Ten Ten Players. Hampton Adams made numerous forays to the Midwest and South to seek funding beyond that which the congregation would be able to provide. Two Disciples agencies, the Christian Board of Publication and the Board of Church Extension, provided significant mortgage support. The task proved daunting, but hope kept the enthusiasm alive.

In the midst of these plans the congregation reached its sesquicentennial. A huge celebration ensued, but as Hampton Adams wrote, "a proud 150-years of increasing service to a community, of constantly bettered religious training for countless people, of ever-growing spiritual development, cannot be capsuled into one week for ready appraisal." The celebration included a pageant of the congregation's history produced by the Ten Ten Players. The choir offered the Verdi "Requiem" in concert and an anthem contest set by church musician Solon Alberti was won by the church's student pastor, Charles W. Wilson, Jr., also a talented musician. Church member Vincent Sardi contributed the celebration dinner from his famed restaurant in Manhattan's theater district. Much was made of the fact that the sesquicentennial celebration was a major impetus for the church's building plans, which (after higher projected costs caused the elimination of a hostel floor for traveling missionaries and a second elevator) would soon begin construction.

To mark the anniversary, James Craig began writing a new history of the congregation, but illness prevented his completing the project. Fortunately Rose Starratt, retired English teacher and member, volunteered to complete the task. The book, *A Sesquicentennial Review of the Park Avenue Christian Church, New York City,* was published by the Bethany Press in 1960 and has been a significant and invaluable historical record.

Hampton Adams and a committed group of church leaders

worked doggedly to procure funding and complete plans for the new building to replace the old unsuitable parish house. Architects ensured that the facade would include as much as possible of the original and that the new addition would reflect the building's architectural integrity. Cold, wet weather and a sizable mortgage could not dampen the members' hopes as construction began on December 10, 1961. John Gibson, chair of the building committee, led the ceremony assisted by Dr. Wilbur Cramblett, president of the Christian Board of Publication, which helped with financing.

By the next September demolition was complete. The construction phase was complicated. Because of limited storage space, almost every piece of building material had to be delivered "just in time" to be installed. Finally in February 1963, the steel framework and concrete work were completed. On May 12, 1963 the cornerstone was placed in the wall, the congregation's second since the cornerstone laying of the 56th Street building exactly a century earlier.

The five-story building and full basement with classrooms, offices, fellowship hall, stage, sexton's apartment, and a large roof-top playground were well built and functional. Perhaps most cherished was a new church parlor named in memory of beloved pastor, Finis Idleman, where on one wall hangs a portrait of Dr. Idleman. Opposite is a large canvas of "Joseph Sold into Slavery by his Brothers" painted by the respected, early 20th century Dutch artist, Johannes Hendricus Jurres. The painting had been given by Mr. and Mrs. Lawrence Phelps Tower in memory of the Rev. Dr. Thomas Reed Bridges, who had been responsible for the sanctuary's construction in 1909, and his wife, Adeline Tower Bridges. Recently restored through the efforts of former trustee Jean Wirth, the painting continues to grace the room. The Idleman Parlor became the setting for countless community coffee hours where generations of worshipers bonded. Several couples recall their first meeting here. In gratitude for the interfaith commitment of the pastor

Silas Shephard became the first regular pastor of the congregation in 1850.

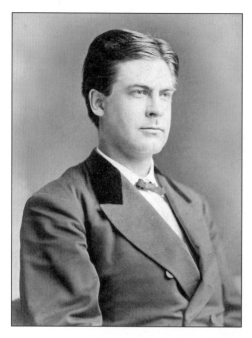

Pastor Joseph Cleaver led the church when it began construction of its first new building on West 56th Street.

Pastor B.B. Tyler was a very popular preacher. His wife Sarah established women's programs at the church.

Pastor Urban Brewer, a champion of the abolition of slavery, led the church for nine years.

The 28th Street location of the church as it currently looks. The building has housed various businesses, including a computer store and now it is a occupied by a wholesaler.

Pastor D.R. Van Buskirk served the church from 1874-1879 and, according to *The New York Times,* was "among the members of the church held in the highest esteem."

Vachel Lindsay often entertained members of the church with the "chanting of his poetry" in the home of Pastor Miner Lee Bates.

The church had one of the most successful and long-lasting Chinese Sunday Schools, which taught immigrants English, promoted Christian values, and offered a place to socialize.

Pastor James Philputt, who served from 1912-1916, had a progressive zeal for Christian Unity.

Pastor Benjamin Q. Denham brought new members to the church and was a champion for social justice. Unfortunately, he was involved in a series of moral issues that caused tension within the church.

The West 81st Street location and the iron gates that Pastor
Finis Idlemen demanded to be opened.

Pastor Finis Idleman served for 25 years. His
spiritual passion brought him overwhelming respect
and love in the church.

The children who were in the first Community House Vacation
Bible School in 1919, led by Miss Merrell (bottom left).

A group on an outing in 1922. That year 80 boys were enrolled in the youth program.

This group of girls from the Community House attended Camp
Burton in Palisades Interstate Park in the early 1920s.

The Sunday School staff from 1922, who were among the 40 people that served the Community House children that year.

Sunday School teacher, Miss Merrell, with a student in the early 1920s.

Eleven different nationalities were represented in this class at
the Community House (circa 1920).

Children participating in May Day festivities in the early 1920s.

In 1944 Meril May was the chair of the committee on expansion and was instrumental in moving the church to the current location on Park Avenue.

The building was purchased in 1944. Originally, it was built by the Reformed Protestant Church of Garden Street and then sold to the Union Presbyterian Church, which later named it Park Avenue Presbyterian Church.

MEMBERSHIP CARD

PARK AVENUE CHRISTIAN CHURCH
(Disciples of Christ)

1010 PARK AVENUE

NEW YORK 28, NEW YORK

"This church defends no doctrine but Christ
Preaches no gospel but love
Has no purpose but to serve."

We strongly urge everyone to become associated with a local church, especially in this city. The church can sustain and bless you. You can reinforce and support the church. Make your decision today to unite with Park Avenue Christian Church.

Please fill in the needed information and bring this card forward to the minister during the singing of the invitation hymn and be received into this fellowship by him. If you wish to talk with the minister before uniting with this congregation, please indicate your request on the reverse side.

Membership Card from the late 1940s.

k the appropriate statement.

faith in Christ and apply for Baptism.
y membership to Park Avenue Christian

member by statement of previous mem-

on the mailing list.
re information about this church and

ference with the minister about church

nister call on me, or on

....

....
Date ....

Name ....
Address ....
.... Telephone ....
Business ....
.... Telephone ....
Present Membership in ....
.... Church
Address ....

Other Information You Wish to Add ....
....
....

Pastor Ira Langston receiving new members.

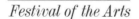

Program for the 1966 Festival of the Arts sponsored by and held at the church.

Pastor Hampton Adams helped create programs for young gang members, promoted interfaith relationships within the community, and was the catalyst for the establishment of the Ten Ten Players.

A production by the Ten Ten Players (now Theatre Ten Ten), which has become one of the oldest Off Off Broadway theatres in New York.

Clementine Miller Tangemen was an elder, philanthropist, and social activist who provided generous financial support to the church.

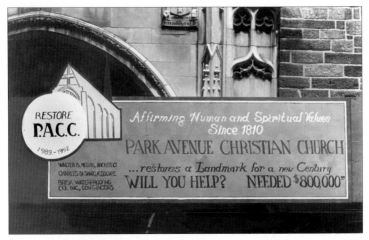

Banner for the church's capital campaign to renovate the historic building.

Restoration work on the exterior of the building.

Sanctuary of Park Avenue Christian Church.

The Park today.

and congregation, Dr. Adams's Jewish friend, Jacob Goldfarb, contributed the cost of the pastor's handsome, mahogany-paneled study.

The fellowship hall's kitchen was an empty room; the equipment in the old kitchen had necessarily been discarded. Three years earlier Colonel Harland Sanders, creator of Kentucky Fried Chicken, while en route to the Edinburgh World Convention of Christian Churches, had attended services dressed in full white regalia. In those years a lunch was served each Sunday; Colonel Sanders enjoyed his meal, but questioned how such delicious food could be prepared with so few resources. Carrie Cooper, the church's beloved caterer, simply replied, "We manage." Complimenting Carrie Cooper that her chicken recipe was "better than mine," and noting that the congregation was planning a new building, Sanders offered to contribute a commercial stove. In 1964 when Sanders returned to New York as a guest on TV's "What's My Line?" and later showed up for church, Hampton Adams gently reminded him of his offer. Colonel and Mrs. Sanders extended their generosity and fully furnished the new, but empty kitchen with restaurant quality equipment.

The choir rehearsal room and office for the organist-choirmaster was named in honor of Solon Alberti, but Hampton Adams resolutely refused the many requests to add his name to a portion of the building. Three years after his death the official board in 1968 unanimously named the entire new structure after him. A bronze plaque near the entrance of the foyer states that the building is "named in loving memory of Hampton Adams, D. D., Pastor 1954 -1965."

Although the cost of a hospitality floor for visitors and church leaders proved prohibitive, the construction of excellent, child-appropriate facilities for the proposed Park Avenue Christian Church Day School was included. The first director, Abbie Lewis, head of St. John's Lower School in Houston, Texas came to organize the school. Coincidentally she was the daughter of

Joseph Bradford Cleaver, pastor of the church from 1878 to 1881. Opening on October 7, 1963, the school's first enrollment was 30, growing through the years to 180 children with 22 teachers. From the outset the school emphasized ethical and moral values but was never intended to inculcate specific religious content. Children in the school are from families of diverse religious and non-religious backgrounds.

Having established the Day School, Abbie Lewis retired after one year. She was followed by Elizabeth Frothingham, who also was instrumental in founding the International Play School of the United Nations. From its beginnings in the church, the International Play School spread across the city and offered pre-school and kindergarten experiences in many cultures and languages. Myrta Ross spoke of it as one of the most meaningful interracial and intercultural mission efforts the congregation could host and support. Children ages four through seven from more than 80 countries have attended the school which had one of its main settings in the church until 2009.

Other directors of the Day School have been Mrs. Thomas J. McGrath (1968-1976) and Lona Tannanbaum (1977). Jean (Mrs. Morris) Wirth, chair of the Day School Committee, led the selection of the longest tenured director, Marcella Wainwright (1977-2006). After a major evaluation in the 1980s, she shared leadership with Nancy Vascellaro (1982-2000) as Director of Education. Betsy Newell is the current Director and Rhonda White is the current Director of Education. Guided play and carefully planned activities prepare the children for the academic emphases of on-going schools, public, private and parochial. Highly respected as one of the better institutions in the city, the school requires that lead teachers have master's degrees in early childhood education.

A quiet but revealing tribute to Hampton Adams is recalled by Jean Wirth. While attending a Christian Women's Fellowship meeting the time came for her to pick up her child Billy at the close of the day. So that she would not need to make energetic

Billy sit through a program that was anything but child-centered, Hampton Adams took Billy for a walk in the park.

In April 1965, Hampton Adams submitted his resignation to retire at age 68. Describing his tenure, he concluded that he "would rather have a call to the ministry of this church than to any other." His well-earned retirement was not to be, for he died suddenly following a visit with friends to the New York World's Fair. His obituary in *Forward* recounted his accomplishments including, his seven books, and especially emphasized his international commitments with the World Council of Churches.

As a tribute to Hampton Adams, and in appreciation for the sanctuary and the people of the congregation, elder Dr. Comer Shacklett produced a handsome, leather-bound, hand-written and illustrated book which pictured and described the stone, wood, and stained and painted glass symbols throughout the church. Unique of its kind, it is a cherished addition to the church library.

In the 1950s and '60s the Park Avenue congregation perhaps numbered its most participants, an estimated 600, 450 of whom held membership. Hampton Adams's significant leadership was enhanced by the flourishing of main-line Protestant churches across America. These were the years when the National Council of Churches in the United States, and its sister program, Church World Service, received significant support from its member denominations, and the staff included a large cadre of Disciples ministers, missionaries, and Christian educators. Many of these have been counted among the congregation.

The church's newsletter, *Forward,* often edited by pastors or staff members, was voluntarily assembled by deacon William C. "Bill" Calhoun, whose good humor and leadership during these years is legendary. The congregation, located at a primary crossroads of the world, counted among its supporters people around the nation and beyond — from Caryl and Dorothy Watkins in Australia to the Dube family in Kenya. *Forward* has been, and continues to be, the cherished communications link for many.

A Daunting Decade

Once again it was in the Midwest, the center of Disciples strength, that the congregation sought another pastor. The search led to the University Place Christian Church in Champaign, Illinois, where Dr. William Jackson (Jack) Jarman, age 48, had served as pastor for 17 years. A graduate "with distinction" from the University of Missouri and New York's Union Theological Seminary, Dr. Jarman served as a Navy chaplain during World War II. His commitment to Disciples historic ecumenical involvements was evidenced in his many appointments, including two terms as chairperson of the Council on Christian Unity and chair of the Disciples delegation to the Consultation on Church Union. Recommendations from Illinois unanimously described him as a "dynamic preacher," calling him "one of the first ten pulpit men in our brotherhood." Jack Jarman's wife, Mary Mona Love Jarman, and two of their three children, Mona Ellen and Mary Denise, joined him in New York as his ministry began in October 1965. Their son Bill, already a student at Bethany College, went on to Yale Divinity School. Both Bill and his wife, Carol Somplatsky, were ordained at the church and in the 1980s, serving as co-chairs of the Community and World Outreach Department, led the congregation to become one of the actively engaged Shalom (peacemaking) congregations of the Disciples of Christ. Today they both serve in mission and environmental justice ministries for the Presbyterian Church (USA).

The Rev. Dr. A. Dale Fiers, president of the United Christian Missionary Society, and later General Minister and President of the denomination, provided significant "bookends" for Jack Jarman's ministry. He delivered the sermon at his installation on November 21, 1965, and thirteen years later served as interim pastor following Jarman's sudden death in 1978.

The tradition of a daunting transition from Midwestern culture to Gotham life continued unbroken. Adjusting to urban Manhattan life proved difficult for family members, and they soon moved from the Riverside Drive apartment that had been the pastor's residence for many years to Teaneck, New Jersey. With the move came the challenge of long daily drives commuting to and from the city.

Although untiring at his work, Jack Jarman's ministry was a new experience for the congregation. Used to the very gregarious personalities of previous pastors, the congregation found that his quiet, unassuming, and almost self-effacing manner sometimes kept relationships distant. Yet individuals who worked closely with him found him warm and supportive. His sermons with titles such as "Religion without Boundaries" were well received and his progressive, ecumenical, and interfaith commitments encouraged the already liberal-leaning community. Student assistants from Union Theological Seminary during his tenure gratefully affirmed the outstanding quality of his preaching. Among these are Peggy Owen Clark who was ordained in the church and later became co-regional minister for the Northeastern Region of the Christian Church (Disciples of Christ), and Regional Minister for the Southwest Region; Joseph Jeter, Jr., today professor at Brite Divinity School; and Richard E. Sturm, continuing elder, regional leader, and professor at New Brunswick Theological Seminary. Dr. Sturm observed that Dr. Jarman's sermons reflected even greater spiritual depth after the untimely death of his talented and artistic wife, Mona, in 1976.

Soon after the launching of the Jarman years challenges to both city and church erupted. The city's fortunes, which always impacted on the strength of the congregation, were declining by the late 1960s. Crime was increasing, the city's finances were bleak, and public services were deteriorating. Like many major U.S. cities, New York suffered race riots, gang wars, and population and industrial decline. Angry activists and minority groups like the Black Panthers and Young Lords took matters into their own hands and organized rent strikes and garbage offensives, demanding justice, and services for the neglected poor. Establishing free health clinics and social programs, various groups sought with some success to bring "Power to the People." Sadly, sometimes with media-hyped exaggeration, the nation began to view New York City as overwhelmed by crime. Congregations would not remain immune.

Student assistant, Joe Jeter, underscored in *Forward* how these events were not isolated from the congregation in his account of an incident in worship: "Those of you [at] church Sunday witnessed one of the tragedies of our time. The young man who wandered into our sanctuary Sunday was named David, who lives in his words 'somewhere in the discord between Edim and D6 [sic].'. . . In the vestiges of a young man with his brain parched and jellified by hallucinogenic drugs is probably a talented, bright young man. . . a very gentle and sensitive person. Good people, pray for David. . . ."

An article in the January 9, 1969, issue of *Forward* offered this somber observation from a meeting of the official board: "A lengthy and deep discussion was had concerning the future of the Park Avenue Christian Church. Anyone who is familiar with the situation in New York City realizes that every church here faces grave problems. In the last five years fifty Protestant churches have closed their doors in Manhattan."

The indebtedness on the Hampton Adams building had become onerous to a declining congregation. A committee, including John R. Gibson, James Royalty, Richard Johnson, Clementine (Mrs. Robert) Tangeman, Nina Boswell, Sybil (Mrs. Ned) Lavengood, and Robert Peterson, was appointed to research the concern and receive suggestions from the congregation. Church membership, always a "revolving door," as Manhattanites have always been extremely mobile,

94

was declining precipitously. Yet a strong biblical "remnant" remained not only loyal but sacrificial in their dedication.

By 1971 the financial crisis deepened. Various options were suggested. Among them federation with nearby Park Avenue United Methodist Church and a "revitalized program." For two years a shared Sunday Church School was organized with the Methodists just around the corner. Other possibilities included: arrange for another congregation to use the facilities for payment of the outstanding indebtedness; sell the property and lease it back for continuing church activities; or sell the property and relocate with another church in their building. Fortunately, none of these options was ultimately required.

The congregation stoically embraced its mission and a number of initiatives were established. Jack Jarman's leadership brought the congregation into a long-standing relationship (including financial) with the Temple of Universal Judaism and its rabbi, Roy Rosenberg. Significant interfaith dialogue was added to the ecumenical agenda. Dr. Jarman's sympathy for the imprisoned was expressed in his leading the congregation to a concern for the incarcerated. Participation in the Fortune Society, a group dedicated to the rehabilitation of former inmates of the prison system, was encouraged.

At the center of Jack Jarman's commitments was his zeal for Disciples' polar star of Christian unity. His leadership among various movements was graphically illustrated by his endeavors to create a true Roman Catholic-Protestant worship experience. Rebuffed by the very conservative New York Archdiocese in his preaching invitation to a Catholic priest, he simply turned to the Sisterhood where two nuns gladly responded and were well received by the congregation.

Congregational leadership was strengthened by the contributions of Wilma and Norwood Tye, former missionary educators in the Philippines. She was the congregation's first woman elder and started a movement which led to a single diaconate for both women and men in 1982.

A source of congregational strength was an enduring worship tradition that supported the spiritual experience so necessary for congregational well-being. A student of historic worship, Jack Jarman's liturgical sensitivities brought depth to services and established a heritage which was gratefully followed in later years.

Spiritual dimensions to worship continued to be enhanced by music ministries. After 35 years Solon Alberti announced his retirement in 1967 as beloved organist-choirmaster and was named Director of Music Emeritus. G. Dene Barnard, Union Seminary graduate of the School of Sacred Music, followed. An outstanding organist who offered recitals throughout the city, he could not perform at the church since the original Robjon organ installed in 1910 had recently "died" and had been replaced by an electronic instrument. Musicians pointed out that the limited quality of the instrument was nevertheless much improved simply because the acoustics of the sanctuary are so excellent. Dene Barnard was followed briefly by Larry Peterson and then by Karen McFarlane in September 1974. Members spoke gratefully of her ability to "reach and touch people musically." She introduced a tradition that continued for two decades — the Advent Celebration of the Nine Lessons and Carols.

Another popular Advent/Christmas tradition that has continued since 1971 is the lovely Hanging of the Greens event that annually transforms the sanctuary for the season. Members of the Book Group were the initiators of the project with consultation from Jean Wirth. The cherished event has continued through four decades.

The Day School grew in enrollment and quality each year. Betsy (Mrs. Cahal H.) O'Malley brought widespread respect for the program from the community, and the school's reputation garnered recognition as one of the best pre-school/kindergartens in the city.

Through the troubled 1970s the congregation endured. They

were shocked and saddened when Jack Jarman suddenly died just before Christmas in 1977. Student associate pastor Richard Sturm was pressed into immediate preaching responsibilities. Insights into Jack Jarman's pastorate were expressed in his Christmas letter written days before his death. "The church is inevitably caught up in the malaise of a great city. . . . The Church can go two ways. One is to succumb to the problems through doing the same old things in the same old way. The other is to reach out for the lonely, frightened, and lost. That is going to take more imagination and hard work than we like. But if there are enough people who care about Christ and what happens to people, that is the way we will take."

Paul A. Crow, Jr., former church member when he was Executive Secretary of the Consultation on Church Union and president of the Council on Christian Unity, spoke at the memorial service on January 3, 1978. He defined Jack Jarman's work as a "herculean ministry in a city and culture where the Church enjoys few of the symbols of visible success." Wilma and Norwood Tye, who offered unstinted leadership during these challenging years, wrote especially of Dr. Jarman's commitment to his family, the ecumenical cause, and to the church.

After Jack Jarman's unexpected death the congregation, distressed and already daunted by the problems of decreasing population and financial difficulties facing the city, steadfastly determined to seek a new pastor. Accurate or not, New York City's reputation had become that of a "crime-ridden relic of history." Two years earlier the city had only avoided bankruptcy through a humbling federal bailout loan and state supervision. One newspaper headlined that the U.S. President had all but declared, "Drop dead, New York!" Hit with the blackout of 1977 and a spate of "Son of Sam" serial murders, city and congregation alike faced depressing challenges. Within the church Clementine Miller Tangeman, whose generous stewardship was accompanied by her willingness to mitigate increasing annual deficits, related plans to move permanently back to her home in Columbus, Indiana, and indicated that her contributions would inevitably decline. Jack Jarman had publicly questioned not only whether the church could survive, but whether New York City itself had a future.

Hope Undaunted

The congregation, never large by Midwestern numbers, by the late 1970s had dwindled to fewer than 100 fully participating members. At Jack Jarman's death major pastoral leadership was thrust into the hands of Richard Sturm, beloved part-time associate working with singles and young adults while he was in the midst of doctoral studies at Union Seminary. In spite of the distressing circumstances, the congregation's stellar history attracted two senior, respected Disciples leaders as interim pastors: C. Curtis Jones, famed pastor and prolific author; and later A. Dale Fiers, retired General Minister and President of the Christian Church (Disciples of Christ). Both endeavored energetically to motivate contributions from friends and former members, so that funds would be available for a what Dale Fiers proclaimed with as much hope as certainty, "a new era of ministry."

Overall administration was a desperate need. Although volunteers gave generously of their time and talent, the tasks were overwhelming. The school alone had twenty-two employees. In June 1978, multi-talented Wesley Livingston was engaged as church administrator. Essential efficiencies were established during his tenure that continued after his retirement in 1990. He was followed by another able professional, Fredricka Cunningham, who added church administrative duties to her other responsibilities, including editor of *Forward* until she retired after serving twenty-four years.

The major obstacle confronting the congregation was the

remaining $400,000 mortgage on the Hampton Adams Building that housed the church's well regarded Day School. Dr. Fiers consulted with Clementine Tangeman, elder, philanthropist and social activist, seeking to find ways to meet this formidable challenge. Together they created plans for a four-year campaign to retire the debt in which she would match dollar for dollar all pledges up to $600. To encourage larger gifts, she would match any contribution of $600 or more on a two-to-one basis.

Clementine Miller Tangeman was the matriarch of her family's Irwin-Sweeney-Miller Foundation and her own Christian Foundation, the sources of her support. Her family included a century of outstanding pioneer Disciples leaders. Her grandfather, Z. T. Sweeney, nationally renowned pastor, author, and historian, was an influential peacemaker among different factions in early 20th century Disciples organizations. One of her childhood memories was the annual pilgrimage with her mother to New York City from Columbus, Indiana, not only for theater, concerts, or museum visits, but to attend as many Sunday church services as possible to hear the "great preachers" of the era. Mrs. Tangeman and her brother, J. Irwin Miller, chairman of the Cummins Diesel Company and the first lay president of the National Council of Churches, were the generous benefactors of many church-related, architectural, and cultural institutions. Their industrialist-philanthropist grand-uncle, William G. Irwin, supported the work of his chauffeur, Clessie L. Cummins, who invented a unique diesel engine design that gave birth to the Cummins Corporation.

Simultaneously the search for a new pastor continued at a time when few Disciples ministers expressed interest in living and working in Manhattan. In late 1978 Paul Crow, president of the Council on Christian Unity who had been an elder when he had lived in the area and served as General Secretary of the Consultation on Church Union, and Nancy Heimer of the Department of Church Women and a former member of the Douglass Boulevard Christian Church in Louisville, together suggested that the congregation consider inviting John Wade Payne (the author of this history), Douglass Church's pastor for eighteen years. It was hoped that, as a graduate of New York's Union Theological Seminary, who had pioneered in helping develop one of the nation's first ecumenical community ministries, he might bring a degree of familiarity with the city and the church's needs and goals.

John Payne's admiration for the congregation had long been established. In the spring of 1958 he was teaching high school in Dallas, his home city, while pursuing graduate studies in English and American literature at Texas Christian University. Hampton Adams, always seeking support for the Park Avenue congregation, briefly journeyed to Texas. He was invited to offer a series of Lenten sermons at the Oak Cliff Christian Church in Dallas, where John Payne was an active member. Following one of the services, Hugh M. Riley, Oak Cliff's pastor, and Hampton Adams corralled John into the pastor's study and launched a vigorous campaign to persuade him to enroll at Union Seminary and to "think about" the profession of ministry. By that fall a surprised John found himself at Union Seminary where he discovered his vocation and would soon meet his art historian wife-to-be, Jensene Godwin, a graduate student at the Institute of Fine Arts of New York University.

The Paynes were married in 1960 and Jensene, an active Presbyterian all of her life, found the Disciples appealing and joined Park Avenue Church, in part because of its open membership practice. The generous hospitality provided to Union students by Hampton and Adelaide Adams, by professor and elder Searle Bates and his wife Lilliath, as well as by Clementine Tangeman, whose husband Robert Tangeman, served on the seminary's church music faculty, created treasured student memories.

Thus, eighteen years later, when search committee members Dr. Comer Shacklett and Jean Houston called, John Payne was intrigued and willing to consider the possibility. After lengthy negotiations John, with his wife, Jensene, and their two children, Wade (14) and Rachel (10), agreed to move to New York City in May 1979. Once again, the pastor of a large, thriving Midwestern congregation would respond to the call of this smaller, historic congregation. Naively, John Payne's seminary memories to some extent blinded him to the city's misfortunes and the congregation's fragility. He remembers that on one occasion of meeting with a group he assumed to be the search committee, he was shocked to learn that the less than 30 people gathered made up most of the active membership. He recalls concluding that the congregation's record of per capita giving was simply amazing (in many ways it was), but that he was unaware that more than half of the contributions were from one individual. Nevertheless, his love and admiration for the church and its people soon overcame all hesitations.

On his arrival he was confronted with the detritus of a prolonged garbage strike, the sidewalks and streets lined with bulging, malodorous plastic bags. Worms had invaded the Big Apple. On his first Sunday in May 1979 fewer than twenty-five people made up the congregation. He remembers that many of his early sermons were based on both a scriptural text and a vision of hope he grasped from the children's story, "The Little Engine that Could." Faith was expressed in "I hope I can" and "I think I can" modes.

Subsequently, the Paynes saw, not discouragement, but action. To transition from the luxury of having had two full-time secretaries in Louisville to none in New York, Ota Lee Russell and Ella Pittwood, both retired, offered their valuable services to help the new pastor. Elder Juanita Shacklett, librarian and author, in order to encourage reading, received approval to install a library in a large vacant room in the Idleman Parlor where the materials would be readily available to everyone at the Sunday coffee hour "mingle." Building chair, the always energetic Luther Mook, installed new shelves and lighting. Juanita delightedly observed that the people "actually checked

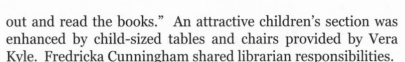

out and read the books." An attractive children's section was enhanced by child-sized tables and chairs provided by Vera Kyle. Fredricka Cunningham shared librarian responsibilities.

Family challenges took precedence for the Paynes. Schools were found for their children, and the congregation rallied around them. But adequate funds for housing had not been anticipated. John Payne was convinced that the only way he could adequately serve would be for the family to live in the congregation's community. But the Paynes' own funds, even combined with the resources of the congregation, fell short. Elder Robert Tesdell and Luther Mook helped search the upper East Side for housing. After many discouragements they located an empty, much deteriorated four-story brownstone house on Lexington Avenue near 94th Street that had been built in 1873 for German immigrant employees of the predecessor of the Ruppert Brewery. The location and price ($126,000) were right. Attorney Morris Wirth, husband of PACC member, Jean, kindly helped the Paynes through the sale. They moved in, but the interior proved to be in far worse shape than it at first appeared. In its heyday, the house had once been the home of Leo Lerman, a well-known writer and magazine editor whose celebrated parties included such famous guests as Truman Capote, Leonard Bernstein, Rudolph Nureyev, and Martha Graham. But by 1979 the house was far from its glory days.

Be it providence or coincidence, at the moment of the Paynes' deepest discouragement, Clementine Tangeman invited them to a gala dance performance by Mikhail Baryshnikov at City College. When she picked them up, the shabby condition of the house in which they were attempting to survive was obvious. The next morning a resolute Mrs. Tangeman was already present in the pastor's study when he arrived. In a no-less-than-life-saving gesture she offered to add the funding of a professional renovation of the building to the matching program she had already established to retire the congregation's debt.

The architectural firm of Hardy, Holtzman and Pfeiffer, with Hugh Hardy supervising, was secured. It would be one year before the $175,000 restoration was complete. Knowing the limitations of the congregation's resources, the Paynes stored most of their furniture and made their "home" in the pastor's study, in various unused rooms in the Adams building, and in the main kitchen. Jensene supervised the restoration, and while it was a supremely daunting experience, the Paynes later looked back and recalled that the time enhanced the family's bonds to each other and the church. The interior of the house was completely rebuilt and an apartment was created for Jensene's elderly mother on the ground floor. The restored home, now the manse, would ensure that the congregation would have a commodious living space for its pastors in its own community, and become a place of hospitality to the congregation. At Mrs. Tangeman's suggestion, the building was named in honor and memory of Searle and Lilliath Bates (who had generously donated an antique Chinese robe, auctioned at Sotheby's, with proceeds contributed to the renovation). Ima Jean Kidd thoughtfully sought and received approval for the congregation to repay the Paynes' initial investment.

Hope was on its way to fulfillment. The "little engine" began hesitantly whispering, "I thought I could." Other good news was demonstrated by the improvement in the city's economy, so that the investment of $300,000 had increased the value of the manse to well over one million dollars. New York was finding its rightful place once again. When Dale Fiers completed his interim in 1979, the basics of the financial campaign worked out with Clementine Tangeman were established. Elder Armand Vergara chaired the program and created the goal, "Debt Free in '83!" The campaign was more successful than many thought possible, and the matching gift possibilities motivated church members and friends from near and far. During this decade leadership of the congregation's board was primarily in the hands of three intrepid women: Evelyn Settle, Evelyn Tesdell, and Myrna Payne. Serving many terms, Preston Davis oversaw the accounts as treasurer.

The "Debt Free in '83" campaign became "The Miracle on 85th Street," breathing new life into the congregation. At the launching of the campaign James Settle spoke for everyone as he described the "near legendary devotion of Clementine Tangeman and the magnanimous generosity of (her) Christian Foundation to this church." By January 1980, *Forward* would announce "Tower To Be Lighted as Victory Is Achieved." Lights in the spire were restored through a special gift by Mrs. DeWitt Brown, Dale Fiers' sister, in honor and memory of her husband, DeWitt Brown, who had died in 1980. On May 4th a large gathering on the roof saw the lights glow once again and scores of helium-filled balloons launched to proclaim victory for the church's venture in faith. Special thanks were offered to Armand Vergara and Ota Lee Russell, who worked tirelessly to promote the campaign. The congregation's gourmet cook, Sarah Mook, with well-loved caterer Carrie Cooper, provided a delicious supper; Jean and Alan Walden were masters of ceremonies; and the church's virtuoso violinist, Dale Stuckenbruck, reached back into his childhood as he played haunting tunes on the saw.

At the 171st anniversary Homecoming, October 11, 1981, the mortgage was burned. The growing choir offered a stunning musical offering of Schubert's "Mass in G." Harry Baker Adams of Yale University, son of Hampton Adams, preached the sermon. Two of the congregation's stalwart leaders from the Idleman years, Merrill May and Lloyd Maxwell, returned. By January 9, 1981 the entire debt plus the renovation costs of Bates House had been eliminated. The congregation gave Clementine Tangeman a thunderous, long, standing ovation in gratitude. Not only the congregation, but also the city, experienced recovery and renewal as the "new era" of the 1980s truly began.

Other serendipities occurred. When the 1910 parish house was razed in 1963 to make way for the Hampton Adams building, a baptistry for immersion provided by the B. D. Phillips family was lost. Tentative plans for a new baptistery had been on hold since 1966 because of a lack of funds. On the first Sunday of John Payne's pastorate a guest worshiper was Mildred Welshimer (Mrs. B. D.) Phillips. Noting with dismay that the church had no baptismal pool she immediately ushered the new pastor into his study and surprised him with a check for $25,000 from the B. D. Phillips Charitable Trust to install one. With this gift, plans were soon drawn for the pool to be placed north of the lectern. When the truck with the fiberglass baptistery arrived outside the church in January 1980, it appeared exotic and strange to New Yorkers, most of whom had no experience of baptism by immersion. A crowd gathered as the children were released from school. A hot tub? A mini-swimming pool? Finally one mother declared, "It is a baptismal pool. I was raised a Baptist and I should know!" The baptistery's oak surface frames six exquisitely carved panels researched and designed by Jensene Godwin Payne that add significant Disciples and ecumenical symbols to the original wood carvings throughout the sanctuary. Sadly, before the completion and dedication of the baptistery on November 20, 1983, Mrs. Phillips had died; representing the family was her nephew, Mark Welshimer.

Although baptism at the "age of accountability by immersion" was the cherished, basic practice of Park Avenue Church, the congregation for decades had offered "open membership" acceptance of Christians baptized in every tradition. The church's progressive commitment to diversity attracted families who, although they understood New Testament practice and supported the Disciples stance, did not find the service of infant dedication fulfilling and needed, emotionally, for their newborns to be baptized. The pastors and elders, not only to support these families, but also because of ecumenical concerns, decided to offer infant baptism on request, but continued to affirm the primacy of Disciples practice. All children were urged to enroll in the Pastor's Classes for full church membership at an appropriate age, and most have been baptized by immersion. As well, numerous individuals and families have been attracted to the congregation because of the practice of immersion.

Soon after the "85th Street miracle," the Trustees, urged by co-chairs Sarah Mook and Clelus Van Raalte, and the pastor, launched the Trustees Fund to build a desperately needed endowment for the maintenance and preservation of the buildings. The Rev. Frank A. Mullen, church member and development professional, chaired the program which by 1985 had raised $175,000. With its sister program, the Ministry and Mission Endowment Fund, the total endowment would grow to nearly $1,000,000 by 2000.

Another endorsement of the congregation's future resulted in the narthex installation of a columbarium. Traditional burials in New York City often required traveling up to 75 miles from the city; many of the city's cemeteries had reached their capacity of burials in graves four deep. With the increase of cremation the city congregation could provide an "urban churchyard" with those related to the congregation enveloped and remembered within the church walls. Jean (Mrs. Howard) Toedter helped establish the handsome bronze and mahogany installation and her husband's ashes were the first placed in the columbarium on the north side of the narthex. The interest has grown; a twin-columbarium has also been placed in the south side. Enhancing the columbarium are unique ceramic vases created by potter-elder Ragnar Naess.

Children's and youth programming, which had thrived after the Hampton Adams Building was completed, had languished during the congregation's and city's difficult years. Now with a pastor who added two young children to the small group already present, the need reopened. It was a continuing hope to involve more Day School families in the congregation. A new priority was established for Christian nurture in 1980. Elder Malcolm Warford, vice president of Union Seminary and parent of two children, recommended Union student, Deborah Jenks, as assistant to help develop children's and youth ministries. Her creative insights and personal warmth brought greater participation of this group in worship and their integration into the whole life of the congregation. After graduation she served in a larger capacity as associate in ministry. Seminary and church relationships continued to be strong. Union seminary student Betty Brewer also worked with the diaconate and in children's ministries. Large paper maché Christmas figures made by the children graced the chancel each Advent for several years.

A significant dimension of the renewal experience in the congregation comes from the nature of New Yorkers themselves. New Yorkers, even on posh Park Avenue, never live in isolation. Economic, social, cultural, ethnic and racial diversity is always apparent. People let each other alone, yet are often compassionate and caring by nature. And, they are also assertive. Thus, each new pastor has discovered that the small numbers of members do not give a true picture of the "size" of the congregation. The congregation has almost no "casual" members; people who worship and work in the church exhibit sturdy commitments. Church members speak their minds and work with their hearts. As he learned this, John Payne sought to offer a ministry based on a theology of hope and change. Nurtured in "process theology," he affirmed that all of life and even the nature of God was changing, and not "the same today and forever." The only constant in life is change, and for a congregation seeking to embrace a new era, this offered a way to embrace the changes needed to fulfill its mission. At first he struggled as he strove to make the transition from a rather stable Midwestern congregation to the more heterogeneous and turbulent urban life, and endeavored to communicate effectively in this unique environment. With time, however, his ministry strengthened. His sermons were published widely, and for over ten years he wrote a column of scriptural exegesis, ideas, and illustrations for *Homily Service,* a magazine published by The Liturgical Conference. At his retirement in 1999 a collection of excerpts from his sermons and Communion prefaces and prayers by Jensene, *A Grace of Seasons,* was published by the church.

The Disciples of Christ/United Church of Christ dialogue

is among the many ecumenical developments endorsed by the congregation. John Payne was appointed to the Ecumenical Partnership Committee of the Disciples and the United Church of Christ, the group assigned to strengthen the ties of the two denominations. With the Broadway United Church of Christ on the West Side, an annual worship service and dinner cultivated a warm relationship between the two communions.

Flourishing Arts

Growth came in many dimensions. Urban mobility slowed numerical growth. The arts provided an exciting thrust throughout the '80s and '90s. Karen McFarlane, organist-choir director since 1974 continued to play the Allen electronic organ. Observing the renewal in the congregation that her generosity had helped to inspire, Clementine Tangeman offered to give the church a new pipe organ. A well-trained violinist committed to church music, Mrs. Tangeman was the editor of the congregation's hymnal of the time, *Christian Hymns,* and the benefactor-founder of Yale University's Institute of Sacred Music. The contract was given to Walter Holtkamp, Jr. of Cleveland, Ohio. The nave placement of the old organ was deemed unsuitable, but its exquisitely carved, Goodhue-designed facade was preserved, and a new, 48-rank tracker (mechanical action) organ was installed in the rear gallery at a cost of $350,000. Mrs. Tangeman dedicated the organ in honor and memory of William Jackson Jarman, "for whom choral and organ music were an essential source of strength and inspiration." A surprise resulted from these arrangements. Karen McFarlane and Walter Holtkamp, Jr., in the course of planning for the organ, developed a relationship that led to their marriage in 1983 and prompted Karen (who moved to Cleveland) to declare, "The church has gained an organ, but lost an organist."

The new organ was dedicated on October 3, 1982 with a year of outstanding recitals by internationally renowned musicians. Extremely talented and only 24 years old, David Higgs was engaged as organist-choirmaster. Under his charismatic leadership, the choir soon overflowed the loft with over thirty members. He also provided energy for the development of a String Ensemble and an enthusiastic Gospel Choir. Estella Pate organized the long-running Recorder Consort, with Joyce Clevenger and Myrna Payne serving the longest. Elaine Cunningham, who served the congregation in many capacities including administrative assistant, assistant organist, choir leader, and later moderator of the congregation, added vocal offerings. The Consort, which also attracted other talented participants from the community, offered a variety of programs including Elizabethan music for productions at Pace University directed by professor and church member Chris Thomas. These developments, added to the ever active Ten Ten Players productions, prompted John Payne to request that a new standing committee on the arts be appointed.

Growing interest in liturgical dance inspired the creation of the church's Dance Network. Elder and Christian educator Ima Jean Kidd invited Laura Hembree, a professional modern dancer with deep grounding in spirituality, to begin working with church members. Pointing out that dance has been a major part of worship in many religious traditions, Ms. Hembree wrote, "At its simplest we see liturgical dance every time we worship – in the patterned movements of the clergy and elders around the Communion table and in the processional and recessional. . . . A worship service is not theater, and the sanctuary is not a stage. Like prayer, music and preaching, dance must be integrated into the service." Soon the liturgical seasons were expressed in creative movement by the Network. The program received national attention when Jensene Payne, program chair for the 1982 Christian Women's Fellowship Quadrennial at Purdue University, invited Ms. Hembree to contribute workshops and dance at the assembly. In 1984 the Dance Network was featured in *The Disciple* magazine and in the 1990s danced each year at the shared Good Friday services at the Roman Catholic Church of St. Ignatius one block south. Later dance leaders included Jan Ford, Wade Payne, Debra Nelson, Kara Miller (who also led dance at two Disciples General Assemblies), Rachel Payne, and most recently, Jessica Wray.

Long time Ten Ten Players leaders handed the reins to a new generation in the 1980s. Musical productions and those designed for children were most successful. Byron Tinsley's "Alice the Magnificent" had two extended runs. The delightful "Dream Princess," written and directed by Bob Cunningham with sets and graphics by Chris Thomas and Randy Seitsinger, regularly sold out. Steve Tapp produced and directed "Silverbeard" with Ten Ten stalwart Jayne Heller providing costumes.

Musical theater and operetta were emphasized when choir soloist Tom Pedersen assumed leadership mid-decade. "The Merry Widow" and numerous Gilbert and Sullivan productions were successfully staged, at times with orchestra. Aspiring actors formed lines down Park Avenue when auditions were announced. In the 1990s the program, while continuing to enlist church members' participation, became a more professional "Actors Equity" theater reflected in the name change to "Theatre Ten Ten." Direction has recently been shared by Lynn Marie Macy, Judith Jarosz, and David Fuller. In 2005 a Fiftieth Anniversary Celebration was chaired by Ima Jean Kidd, Carmon Caplinger, and Jayne Heller. Jayne compiled a history of the group published by the church. Entitled *Theatre Ten Ten Playbill,* it describes all of the productions and lists many of the actors, directors, and supporters of the theater (it is available through the church library and archives).

After two wonderful years David Higgs reluctantly resigned to pursue a career which would ultimately be fulfilled as a renowned concert artist and as professor at the Eastman School of Music. Now with a major organ to attract musicians, more than sixty applications were received for the post. McNeil Robinson, an established concert organist and composer famed for his improvisations, was the congregation's next director of music from 1984 until 2008. Worshipers were especially moved by his responsive Psalm settings. Under his leadership the choir transitioned into more of a professional performance group, and volunteer participation declined. Special services such as Christmas Eve, Ash Wednesday, and the Great Vigil of Easter were the settings for major musical offerings under his guidance.

As more artists joined the congregation, expressions of the arts in worship burst forth, building on a long tradition. For many years in the late 20th and early 21st centuries during Holy Week a unique and spiritually profound service based on the "stations of the cross" was offered by church-member renowned artists. James Teschner's immense, somber, abstract, and numinous paintings surrounded the sanctuary, lighted by Chris Thomas and Dale Abel. Insightful, contemporary interpretations of the Calvary journey were written and read by widely published poet and elder Jack Anderson. Organist McNeil Robinson responded with haunting musical improvisations. In later years the organ portion of the service was replaced by liturgical dance.

When professional woodwind instrumentalist and composer Phil Chester and his family became members of the congregation an opportunity to offer outstanding Jazz worship became another continuing expression of creativity. Phil and his cadre of musicians regularly fill the sanctuary with poignant depth as well as ecstatic joy.

The outstanding organ enabled the church to offer a unique opportunity to another Disciples-related institution, Texas Christian University. The organ department chaired by Emmet G. Smith had developed a nationally recognized reputation for excellence. At John Payne's suggestion, a coveted New York recital was offered to the outstanding senior organ student selected by Professor Smith each year.

 Park Avenue Christian Church

Leadership across the arts spectrum was provided by an active committee on the arts ably chaired by neuroscientist, elder Margaret Rice, whose insight and leadership has been crucial in pastoral and personnel relationships.

Chapter 3

Inspiring
*The Church in the Late
20th Century and Beyond*

"The prophet's call is to claim the entire city as our parish."

— *Pastor Alvin Jackson*

Stabilization and Renewal

John Payne's experience as a teacher fostered his commitment to early childhood nurture. While the Day School has always been a major church program, it had functioned rather independently for a number of years. To strengthen the relationship he scheduled a series of interviews with lead-teachers. He discovered that while the school was well regarded in the community, the faculty desired guidance in implementing a cohesive curriculum. With leadership from and support by concerned parents (especially Linda Chen Bell, Betsy Miller and Donna Vaughn), the church's official board contracted with the School of Education at New York University to pursue a full year's evaluation of the school's program. Energetic leadership was provided by two concerned Day School Committee chairs, the Rev. Dr. Malcolm Warford and Elizabeth Eveillard. The evaluation team led by Dr. Irene Shagaki recommended that the direction of the school be more clearly focused and strengthened. As a result, Nancy Vascellaro was selected by the faculty and committee for a new position of Director of Education, collegial with the director, Marcella Wainwright, whose main responsibilities were administrative, evaluating applications, and placement in on-going schools.

As a result, teachers were evaluated regularly, and annual contract renewals were no longer routine. Periodic consultations of the pastor with the two directors became an administrative priority. The curriculum began to reflect an outreach mission priority of the church: to introduce the children to the diverse economic, ethnic, and cultural nature of communities in New York and in the world. Relationships with parents, which had sometimes been adversarial, improved significantly.

The interfaith relationship established by Jack Jarman between the congregation and the Temple of Universal Judaism flourished. John Payne, working with the temple's rabbi, Roy Rosenberg, and Catholic priest, Peter Meehan, co-wrote

Happily Intermarried: Authoritative Advice for a Joyous Jewish-Christian Marriage, published by McMillan in 1984. The church-temple became the setting for increasing numbers of interfaith weddings led by the two clergymen. John Payne also wrote curriculum materials for Disciples committed to deepening Jewish-Christian understanding.

The two institutions created an annual community service embracing the interracial and interfaith contributions of the Rev. Dr. Martin Luther King, Jr. and Rabbi Abraham Heschel. This remarkable and unique experience, perhaps for the first time anywhere, wove together the Jewish Motsi and Kiddush sharing of bread and cup with the Christian Eucharistic Communion service in a tradition of mutual respect. A later addition has been the awarding of the annual Heschel/King Award of Interfaith Activism. It has become an annual community event enhancing Jewish-Christian relationships which *The Daily News* called "a faithful convocation of remembrance and reunion."

Following the death in 1984 of Mabel Godwin, Jensene Payne's elderly mother, the ground floor apartment in the Searle and Lilliath Bates manse became available. This offered the congregation a new opportunity. Because the cost of housing alone in Manhattan could exceed a typical annual salary elsewhere, it had been assumed that calling a needed associate pastor was not financially viable. The one-bedroom apartment could not accommodate a family with children, but a single individual or couple could live there comfortably.

Becky Hebert, mother of two grown daughters, Yvonne and Rachel de Cordova, and recent honor graduate of Brite Divinity School at TCU, was called and served as associate minister from 1985 until 1988. Her ministries included Christian nurture, peacemaking, justice and feminist concerns, and a large investment in pastoral counseling. Her special gifts were an emphasis on a story-telling approach to preaching and developing "creative visioning" emphasizing the imagination. She has since served as campus minister at the University of

Oklahoma, and at congregations in Minnesota and Missouri.

Up Against It

Even though the city was economically and culturally thriving in the 1980s and early '90s, two almost overwhelming challenges haunted the city and its religious/humanitarian institutions: the AIDS crisis and increasing homelessness. Thousands, including many talented and creative individuals, became victims of the HIV-AIDS pandemic. Nearly all of the memorial services conducted in these decades were for those who died before long-term medical therapy became available. Outstanding musicians, editors, counselors and ordained pastors – some of the congregation's true saints – succumbed to the disease. Church members rallied and actively worked for better political and social support for the ill and dying.

The AIDS crisis only complicated the increasing numbers of homeless people living on the streets. Homelessness, which has been present across much of America for decades, becomes even more visible and pervasive in urban areas such as Manhattan. Since the early 1990s few nights have passed without homeless "guests" sleeping under large cardboard sheets on church steps throughout the city. Park Avenue Church, located on one of the wealthiest streets in the world, is no exception. The congregation and trustees had mixed responses to the situation, but concluded that these children of God must not be turned away unless they posed a threat to others or themselves. On more than one occasion John Payne met with residential groups and was grateful to discover that, while some neighbors noisily complained, most understood that a church could not send people away.

The city provided beds and bedding to churches and synagogues which had space available for sleeping quarters. Park Avenue Church with its large school was not prepared to offer this service, but members volunteered to provide security by spending the night in churches where the beds were located. Jane Hovey, chair, and the Mission-Outreach Department explored other possibilities. Because the church was fortunate to have a large, well-equipped kitchen, perhaps a needed food program would be feasible. The church had long supported the community-based Yorkville Common Pantry which distributed food to the hungry and homeless. However, it seemed daunting for volunteers alone to provide meals for what would likely be over a hundred people week after week. But compassion overcame discouragement and anxiety. At an inspired moment in a frustrating meeting, Jane Hovey, with the strong, vocal support of David Schmauch, declared, "Let's do it!" The Saturday Community Lunch Program for the hungry and homeless was launched in 1989 with a small cadre of volunteers. For the first few years David Schmauch prepared many of the meals with Jane Hovey organizing the volunteers. Soon others from nearby institutions added support: Park Avenue United Methodist Church, Manhattan Church of Christ, the Temple of Universal Judaism, and the Roman Catholic Church of St. Ignatius, Loyola. The program has continued for twenty years. In more recent years Henry Hewes has prepared many of the meals.

While alleviating hunger has been the priority, far more support is needed for hungry and homeless people to become self-supporting. When elder Rev. Wayne Reed invited the guests of the Saturday Community Lunch Program to begin meeting weekly, about twenty responded. They were encouraged to share personal stories from their lives on the street in order to bond and assist one another. Asked to name themselves, they chose "Exodus," because "we're crossing over to a better place" of employment and housing. By 1998 the group was "giving back" to others by taking responsibility to cook and serve the Saturday meal. Led by Alton DuConge, who has become a permanent cook, and supported by church members, they worked together for seven years. Ultimately the Exodus Group permanently changed the culture of the program. First, those being served began to contribute to the program themselves. Second, because guests themselves were serving, they became a part of the church's outreach program creating a climate of welcome not previously seen. And, third, the group so enlarged the lunch program that it became a bounteous feast both in quantity and quality. The Exodus Group has been cited as a creative way an institution can help mitigate the depression so often associated with hunger and homelessness.

In the early years of these challenges the congregation was again searching for an associate pastor. Allen V. Harris, who had grown up in New Mexico, succeeded Becky Hebert in December 1989 after a long search process and evaluation of the definition of a valid candidate for ministry. Allen graduated with honors from Phillips University and TCU's Brite Divinity School, where his major professor named him as "one of the three top students in the past 18 years." He had excellent recommendations from the supervisor of his student pastorate and stood out among the candidates with one exception: he was openly gay and thus denied ordination by the Disciples Southwest Region. For the search committee the concern was not his homosexuality. Most of the congregation had long quietly embraced gay members as leaders. Biblical scholar Richard Sturm and John Payne had each preached in support of full acceptance of homosexual persons as completely compatible with Christian teaching. Nevertheless, a call would be groundbreaking. No major Disciples congregation had yet appointed an openly gay pastor to its staff; no regional ministry had yet supported the ordination of openly gay or lesbian candidates.

In an exhaustive interview with the search committee Allen related that his homosexuality was an integral part of his humanity, but that his "calling and cause is Christ," not his sexual orientation. Concerns among the committee included possible negative responses of some church members, parents in the church's Day School, and the community. Ultimately the committee responded positively to the pastor's suggestion that if a better candidate for the job were to be found, they would dismiss Allen's candidacy, but if he were indeed the best candidate, his sexual orientation should not be a barrier.

In a series of small group conversations with Allen Harris, members of the congregation came to appreciate his sense of vocation, experience, moral integrity, and fitness for ministry. When the decision was made to approve his calling, no dissenting votes were cast. Only two members left, and the fears of rejection by Day School parents proved groundless. On the contrary, some parents chose the school because of the church's openness and diversity.

However, difficult and divisive work lay ahead. The Park Avenue congregation had been a major contributor of leadership and funds to the Northeastern Region of the denomination. For Allen to be called as a recognized minister of the Disciples of Christ, the Northeastern Region had to approve him as a candidate for ordination.

Dr. Richard Sturm has made an extensive analysis of the ensuing conflict. For insight into the complexities of this process it is necessary to consider the relationship of a congregation to the region in Disciples of Christ polity. While congregations are to a large extent autonomous, nevertheless basic, denominationally defined, and strong covenantal relationships have been long-established among them. One of the glories of the Northeastern Region in the past was the "glimpse of the whole family of God" when Hispanic, Haitian, African-American, and Anglo Disciples, including the Park Avenue congregation, worshiped and worked together. But these covenants are strained when different theological and cultural emphases confront one another. For many congregations the "polar star" of a Christian union that embraces freedom and diversity is paramount. One result has been the virtual union of the Disciples of Christ and the United Church of Christ congregations in the western area of the northeast. However, the culture and thought prevalent among many (but not all) of the Hispanic, Haitian, and African-American congregations emphasized a desire to return to (restore) a perceived purity in the earliest, New Testament church. In these communities embracing diversity of thought and culture can be unsettling. The Park Avenue congregation's commitment to Christian unity and inter-cultural diversity through the Northeastern Region has been evident in their generous investments in the founding of congregations with different ethnic and language backgrounds from their own. Members who served in Regional ministry in recent years include Richard Sturm, Robert Tesdell, Ima Jean Kidd, Bess Terry, Margaret Rice, Wayne Reed, Chris Ney, Myrna Payne, John Lau, Mark Johnston, Belva Brown Jordan, and John Payne.

These tensions focused themselves in the primary responsibility placed in the Region for approving candidates for ordination, including Allen Harris. The Regional Commission on the Ministry assigned to approve ordinations had been divided into three different geographic sub-committees because of the size of the region. The Metropolitan New York division of the committee was evenly divided regarding Allen's candidacy solely because of his sexual orientation. Regional minister Charles Lamb, who cherished diversity, and Paul Rivera, lay Hispanic leader who was chair of the Metro Commission on the Ministry at the time, offered the possibility of a solution by consulting with the other two sub-committees so that a decision would reflect the action of the full Commission on the Ministry. After numerous meetings, Allen's ordination was ultimately approved in 1991. The fallout from these tensions continue. Paul Rivera later became moderator of the Christian Church (Disciples of Christ), but his reconciling witness eventually led to his being rejected by other Hispanic leaders in La Convencion; he now worships in another denomination.

Two years later the congregation elected to become Open

and Affirming (see page 128). Sadly, many of the Hispanic congregations all but severed their relations with the Park Avenue Church, the region's largest contributor and supporter. Richard Sturm, who gave unstinting energy and leadership to the region, also faced rejection along with several others from the congregation. Park Avenue has had little choice but to invest its mission in other Disciples of Christ ministries. Attempts to open dialogue and bridge the differences have often been received from the General Church, which helped the Region to call Mary Anne Glover as Interim Regional Minister in 2008, with the hope that her leadership may provide enough stability for the Region to determine its future.

The challenge, however, invigorated the congregation with purpose. Allen and his life-partner, the Rev. Craig Hoffman, a minister of the United Church of Christ, settled into the ground floor apartment of Bates House, and the two families – the Paynes and the Harris-Hoffman family – bonded as good neighbors with strong filial relationships. In his early years in New York, Craig served as chaplain at a housing facility supporting individuals living with HIV-AIDS in Greenwich Village. Allen brought an enlarged commitment and leadership to public justice and human liberation as well as strong pastoral skills. With the counsel and support of an active Pastoral Relations Committee John Payne and Allen Harris developed a valued collegial ministry, sharing many responsibilities, including worship leadership, preaching, and membership development. Allen, working with excellent church school leaders, Melissa Little, Jana Nordquist, and Rachel Payne, helped children's ministries to thrive.

The confidence of the congregation in Allen Harris was widely affirmed. Two national Disciples magazines published his articles, one about "growing up gay," and the other, "Why should the church ordain openly gay men and lesbians?" He was elected to the Disciples' General Board and Administrative Committee in 1999. That same year his commitment to justice led him to an act of civil disobedience and arrest (no charges made) in a major New York City demonstration with more than 1,700 others protesting the police killing of young, unarmed Amadou Diallo.

The Christian Church (Disciples of Christ), because of its ecumenical commitment, has provided a large percentage of the staff of the National Council of Churches of Christ in America. Many of these, as well as seminary students and faculty and other church professionals, have enhanced the life of the congregation. Twenty-three ordained ministers were counted among the congregation in the mid-1980s. In 1989, in the midst of a sabbatical, Ima Jean Kidd sparked a creative development. These men and women were invited to form a group of Pastoral Partners, sharing their particular expertise and experience by serving as volunteers in professional ministry. The first Pastoral Partners were Ima Jean Kidd for hospitality, Richard Sturm for Biblical studies, and Sally S. Bailey for spiritual nurture and "healing services." Later Partners included Thomas Farrington for theological inquiry, Wayne A. Reed for social justice, and Gerry Brague for contemporary culture. Each offered programs and classes. The Pastoral Partners proved their mettle when for three months the group assumed full pastoral responsibilities following the resignation of Allen Harris as acting senior minister in 2000.

The hospitality emphasis, long a hallmark of the Park Avenue Church and led by Ima Jean Kidd was enhanced by offering an affordable studio apartment in the church to transient visitors. Later this was expanded to a three-bedroom facility "the Little Place in the Park," now closed, named for a generous gift from Melissa Little. In addition, many young people from congregations across the nation recall their introduction to New York City culture and especially to the United Nations when they "camped" in the fellowship hall. This was made more comfortable by the addition of showers, funded by Vera Kyle.

More Challenges, More Progress

During the last decades of the 20th century both New York City and the congregation became more secure. Services improved markedly and people found Manhattan life appealing and expensive. But church life was never without challenge. When sexton Jorge Guevara walked in the door carrying slate roof tiles which had plunged dangerously to the sidewalk, the trustees immediately authorized an architectural survey. The services of architect Walter Melvin and associate Charles Disanto were secured to assess building conditions. In many ways the magnificent 80-year-old sanctuary had stood the tests of time. But loosening roof tiles were only a fraction of the problem. Manhattan schist (crystalline rock) used for the construction of the building had been quarried from the excavations for the subway tunnels. Rain and air pollution had eroded many of the stones which were slowly defoliating to "pie crust." The walls looked solid but a firm poke would cause about ten percent of the stones to crumble. The towering east and clerestory windows had begun to bulge and twist from years of settlement and vibration from nearby train tunnels.

Because of the extensive nature of the restoration process, as well as financial necessity, the work was divided into phases. In 1990 work on the stone exterior began, and later the stained glass windows were restored so that the tasks were substantially completed in 1993. Worship services continued even though the church building was completely surrounded with scaffolding inside and out for nearly four years. Although a line of credit had been established by the trustees through the Disciples Board of Church Extension, the daunting financial challenges were fully met with generosity by hundreds of members and friends in a campaign chaired by Frank Mullen. John Payne recalls being overwhelmed when Clementine Tangeman, as she was wont to do, arrived unexpectedly in the pastor's study and informed him that she would make a grant of $1,000,000 to the project in honor and memory of her family through her foundation. Interest from the Trustees Fund Endowment contributed $160,000.

Because the original architect, Bertram Goodhue, was inspired by the Sainte Chapelle in Paris, the building has an extravagant amount of stained glass, nearly all of which required repair. Major support of the stained glass restoration was provided through creative "Adopt a Window" contributions, from which the biblical symbols in each window were repaired. A booklet published by the church describes the restoration process, names each of the donors, and is available in the archives and church library.

The restoration was not without some heart-stopping moments. Many of the Tiffany window panels were moved to the Rohlf stained glass studio in Westchester County. While stored there, one of the company's trucks was accidentally driven through a wall where many of the panels were awaiting repair. On seeing the shards scattered across the studio John Payne could only think of corpses laid out in a morgue. At first the traumatic loss seemed irredeemable. However, with the expertise of conservator, Arthur Femenella, and the skills of the craftsmen at Rohlf Studio, shards of smashed glass were "end glued," new leading was installed, and the special qualities of Tiffany layered glass were painstakingly restored. Ultimately less than five percent of the glass had to be replaced. The results were breathtakingly beautiful, as vibrantly luminescent as they were in 1910.

In the course of restoration it was observed that some of the finest glass of the east Tiffany window had been hidden behind the organ when it was installed in 1982. Four of these panels were removed, installed, and lighted in the blind empty niches of the south aisle to balance windows in the north aisle. Because of their proximity to worshipers in the nave, the unique Tiffany fabrication of faceted glass can be observed. Finally, the organ, though completely covered with plastic, was inundated with dust. A second grant from Clementine Tangeman, the organ's donor, contributed the entire cost of cleaning and repairs to the organ.

The final cost of the restoration project, the largest investment ever made by the congregation, totaled more than $1,800,000. In a letter to the congregation the pastors recalled that it had been sometimes asked, "Why on earth would a middle-sized congregation of Christians invest nearly ten times their annual budget to restore their building?" They offered many answers. It is "on earth" that God's activity and presence are revealed. Our landmark church building with its high arches and spire proclaims God's presence in this tall-towered metropolis. They counseled naysayers to note that, if our building were no more, our mission and all of our programs would be "homeless." It is worth remembering that humanity reflects its "image of God" most revealingly in its unique ability to create beauty and wonder. Jesus himself reminded stingy disciples that the costly ointment in the lovely alabaster box that was poured over his head was a gift of devotion and love (Matthew 26:7). A congregation's sanctuary is no less.

While the restoration of the building was in progress, the congregation continued to live out its mission. The commitment to embrace diversity, for decades central to its ideology, was affirmed officially in May 1992. The elders' Open and Affirming Statement, encompassing every dimension of the human community, was unanimously approved by the congregation and became a model for many other congregations. The declaration, which evolved over time, and combined into the congregation's mission statement now reads:

> The purpose of this congregation is: to proclaim the gospel of Jesus Christ in worship, sacrament and service, in faithful response to God's will and purposes; to journey in faith, bringing the gospel message, especially that of peace, justice, and the care of God's creation, to bear upon society;

to sustain and be sustained by the general and regional manifestations of the Christian Church (Disciples of Christ); to work cooperatively with Christians in other communions; to seek the oneness of the body of Christ; and to promote interfaith understanding.

Our purpose is further affirmed in this congregation's commitment to Christ's call to love God with all that we are and our neighbor as ourselves. To that end this congregation is open to and affirming of all people whatever their gender, race, age, culture, ethnic background, sexual orientation, religious tradition, economic circumstance, family configuration, or difference in ability. We honor other holy histories and respect those who profess no faith or have chosen different paths to the sacred. We affirm the love of Christ in our lives, and we welcome everyone into this community and invite them to share in its life and ministry. In response to the grace which Christ has given to us, we glorify God, we commit ourselves to growth in the spirit, and we rejoice in the worth, gifts, and dignity of every person as a child of God.

The sentence which affirms that the congregation "will honor and respect all holy histories and paths to the sacred" voiced a growing, new approach to the Christian faith. While firmly holding to the centrality of Christ in their own lives and a commitment to share that faith enthusiastically, the congregation affirmed that they would honor other historic faith traditions and embrace the people who affirm them.

GLAD, the national Gay Lesbian and Affirming Disciples organization, encouraged the Open and Affirming movement within the denomination, and the New York GLAD organization met often in the church facilities. Having stated the traditional openness of the congregation as a mission statement, the church started other groups to explore the possibilities and limitations of openness in a Christian context.

Support of young, energetic seminarians as student assistants was confirmed once again by the arrival of Rachel Frey, president of the student body at Princeton Theological Seminary. She engaged in the social activism commitments of the church, especially in community outreach, and brought a renewed emphasis to the congregation's "Shalom" (peace-making) commitments. Nationally the Disciples of Christ established two "discernment" priorities for study and action: Racism and the Authority of Scripture. The Park Avenue congregation, after petitioning the General Board to add the Role of Gay and Lesbian Persons as the third discernment priority, was invited to send representatives to speak to the Administrative Committee. Deacons Diane Paulsell and Matthew Chisholm were selected and made major presentations. Diane, the parent of an eighteen-month-old son, spoke of her hopes for the process. "I want to raise my son in a church where people talk honestly about inclusion and where he will learn that church is really for everyone. I want him to know that no matter who he turns out to be, he will have a place at the table." Matthew Chisholm, a hospital administrator in a committed gay relationship for eight years, recalled the church's journey to become Open and Affirming and concluded, "I'm not able to adequately express in words, just how degrading it is for me to be asked to try to change the very nature of who I am as a person... how painful it feels, to have the loving, committed, and monogamous relationship that's given me so much happiness... derided as something sinful and ugly." He concluded, given "our passion for justice and willingness to love, I can't help but be optimistic about our ability to work together toward [the discernment process]."

It was not to be; the concern did not become a subject for discernment. Yet the discussion continues, the positive responses grow, and they obviously won't go away. To the congregation it is a question of simple justice.

An idea germinated by Walter and Jo Ann Ashley resulted in the formation of the Thomas Discussion Group. The name reveals the purpose: like the "doubting" disciple Thomas, people were urged to raise, research, and discuss the questions "everyone feels but are reluctant to ask," especially in the church. Using contemporary theological writings, novels, drama, and film, the participants often discovered their faith enhanced in the midst of their often all-but-unanswerable questions.

The "turnaround" experienced by the city and the church in the 1980s continued through the end of the century. Growth was slow but steady; participation grew more than four-fold in these decades. Increased stewardship accompanied by larger income from the church's Day School and other groups using the church's facilities brought more stability. The pastors and trustees had long sought to make the institution less dependent on the generosity of Clementine Tangeman, whose annual contributions would at times approach 50 percent of the people's stewardship. While members and friends increased their annual giving, so did Mrs. Tangeman by simply augmenting her pledge to equal the annual budget's percentage increase. In many of these years a small surplus meant that escrow funds for building maintenance and the trustee's and mission and ministry endowments also increased. John Payne had begun his pastorate with two financial convictions. First, that it was quietly and perhaps unconsciously tempting for members to assume that the benevolence of a few individuals would "take care of the church" and that they could be somewhat less generous in their stewardship. Many leaders sought to change this understanding and build better annual giving. The second conviction was related. Because of costs not experienced by suburban congregations, the congregation could not continue to exist on annual giving alone. A significant endowment was a necessity and was very slowly building, growing to nearly $1,000,000 by the close of the 20th Century; this was helpful, but still quite inadequate. A number of families and individuals including the church in their wills has steadily increased the endowment.

Clementine Tangeman put to rest any assumption that she and her foundation would ensure the congregation's future financially. Approaching her 90th birthday, she informed the pastor that she and her family did not think it wise to endow congregations. Each generation, she stated, should support its own mission, ministry, and facilities. Aware that a sudden drop in her giving would likely be impossible for the members to defray quickly, she pledged that, following her death, her annual contribution would continue for a period of ten years, decreasing 10 percent each year. She died in 1996. This carefully planned approach confronted the congregation with their responsibility and gave them the opportunity to step up to the challenge.

The relationship of John Payne and Allen Harris to each other and to the congregation led to their being considered as simply the pastors, one older, one younger. Jensene Payne, for fifteen years an academic administrator at Hunter College, retired in 1998. That same year as John Payne approached age 66, he announced his retirement for the next February, after almost twenty years. He requested that no retirement gift be made, but that any contributions be designated for special needs of the congregation. A "Payne Appreciation Fund" raised almost $130,000 which made possible a significant addition to the Ministry and Mission Endowment Fund; the air-conditioning of the parlor, fellowship hall and choir room; and a new audio system for the sanctuary. Since the church had sponsored a workshop to help people understand and create examples of ancient Greek and Russian Orthodox iconography, an exquisite icon of the Nativity was commissioned from artist Patricia Miranda and presented to the Paynes by moderator

Ann Canady and Pastoral Partner Thomas Farrington at their retirement dinner. Shortly thereafter the Paynes moved to southwest Florida, Jensene's home state, but are often in the city visiting their childrens' families and the church.

Allen Harris was named "acting senior minister" and was joined for ten months by Allan Lee, former member and retired General Secretary of the World Convention of Churches of Christ, as interim pastor. Sally Bailey, Pastoral Partner for Spiritual Development, moved from volunteer to the staff position of Associate Minister, and provided extensive pastoral services. A search committee, led by artist-potter and elder Ragnar Naess, began a long exploration of various possibilities for ministry. Allen Harris continued as Acting Senior Minister for one year. He loved the congregation and was cherished by the people. But he determined that, while he was able to fulfill the administrative responsibilities of the senior minister for the church and school, these duties were not central to his call to ministry. He and Craig Hoffman moved to Cleveland, Ohio where Craig serves on the national staff of the United Church of Christ. In 2001, Allen became the pastor of the Franklin Square Christian Church serving in an energetic, renewing ministry of another historic congregation.

The New Century: Transition and Trauma

Pastoral changes are always challenging. A retirement and resignation in the course of one year were the catalyst for the congregation to take a long, hard look at itself. Financially stable, but only for a limited number of years following Clementine Tangeman's death in 1996, the congregation needed renewed stewardship and expert leadership on many fronts. Arriving in 2000, intentional interim pastor Suzanne Webb, with excellent experience and expertise, brought a caring and thoughtful ministry. Ragnar Naess continued as chair of the committee for on-going pastoral leadership. Complicating the process, Marcella Wainwright announced her retirement as the longest serving director of the Day School. Controversy over the new director selection process led to the resignation of the other school executive, Nancy Vascellaro, the respected education director. A positive solution came about when Betsy Newell, the former director of the American School in Switzerland (where she continues to direct a summer program) and of New York's International Play Schools, agreed to step in as interim director. Well received by faculty, parents, and congregation, she now continues as the permanent director. Rhonda White is the education director.

Eclipsing all of these challenges, the 9/11 tragedy traumatized city and congregation. Fortunately, no one from the church or school was among the victims, but almost everyone was touched by the death or injury of family members and friends. Services of remembrance, hope, and peacemaking followed; contributions poured in. Everything from protective masks and hard hats to flowers, poetry, and prayers were anonymously placed before the church doors. Suzanne Webb gratefully recalled that the generosity of other Disciples churches and Week of Compassion funds made possible the daily opening of church doors for prayer, solace, and companionship, a needed ministry only sporadically possible in the past. The church continues to be open today, guests are encouraged to enjoy the sanctuary, and a walking tour brochure guides them through the sacred space.

Following a long and intense search, in July 2002, Dr. James "Bo" Crowe was selected as senior pastor and moved to New York with his wife, Christine, and their young son, Jamie. He began serving in September. Suzanne Webb, who had been a stabilizing presence, accepted the call as Interim Regional Minister for the Christian Church in Ohio and now serves as pastor of the Union Avenue Christian Church in St. Louis.

"Bo," as he likes to be called, grew up in the Baptist church, received his Ph.D. in religious studies from Rice University, and taught at the university level for a number of years. He was attracted to the Disciples because of their openness and freedom. Prior to his call to the Park Avenue Church he served as pastor of the United Congregational Christian Church in Lodi, California, where, immediately after the 9/11 tragedy, he was one of the first to organize classes to help people understand the Muslim faith. He brought an inquiring, exploratory faith, and a strong commitment to social justice and interfaith dialogue to his ministry. With Amy Gopp, seminary intern, and supported by the congregation, Bo offered his energy to the Disciples Justice Action Network, a movement committed to alleviate poverty and promote ecology and liberation.

Richard Sturm characterized Bo Crowe's sermons as insightful, prophetic, and "often poetic." Always exploring new paths, when the Temple of Universal Judaism began to remove their booth of boughs set up in the chancel for their Sukot harvest festival, Bo quickly stopped them, declaring the booths to be an inspiration for his Sunday sermon. The Shalom, peacemaking concerns which generated weekly prayer services during the first Gulf War were renewed as a focus of the Sunday prayers for those who have died serving in Iraq and Afghanistan.

Many appreciated his sermons and leadership, including his faith-exploring, justice-seeking nature, and his openness to diverse spiritual paths. However, following a series of discussions with the elders and leaders, Dr. Crowe's column in *Forward* concluded, "About a year and a half into our shared ministry, we became aware of some tensions in the pastor/congregation relationship; differences in perspective on: leadership style, philosophy of ministry, and preaching." Dr. Crowe's strong belief that pastor and people need to be "intimately compatible," led to his tendering his resignation to moderator Elaine Cunningham effective January 2006. Today he serves as senior minister of the Overland Park Christian Church in the Kansas City area, a vital congregation with an effective ministry and mission.

Concerns and changes occurring during the first decade of the 21st century brought the ups and downs of the congregation to another low point. Attendance and participation dropped precipitously. Yet leadership never appeared to flag. A pastoral and nurturing ministry was offered by minister-elder Dr. Judith Hoch Wray during these years, contributing an increased emphasis on inclusive language in liturgy. The congregation's justice-seeking leadership was recognized as both she and Richard Sturm were invited to serve on the Disciples' General Board. Once again, a respected Disciples leader, The Rev. Dr. Chris Hobgood, retired General Minister and President of the denomination, agreed to step in as interim minister. He knew the congregation well, having served earlier as a reconciling consultant to the Northeastern Region in the midst of the "Open and Affirming" conflict. Experienced in pastoral and nurturing ministries, he brought energetic preaching and insight to the congregation's programs and was helpful to the search process led by Melissa Little.

DisciplesWorld magazine in July 2006 aptly summarized the thinking behind the congregation's decision with the headline, "New York congregation, Jackson will make a fresh start together." Alvin O'Neal Jackson, former pastor of the Mississippi Boulevard Christian Church in Memphis and later of the National City Christian Church in Washington, D.C., was recommended as senior pastor. Melissa Little declared, "Jackson is exactly what the church is looking for, from his awe-inspiring pulpit presence to his vision of the church as a beloved community of diverse members." A native of Laurel, Mississippi, Jackson had recently returned to the South following the devastation of Hurricane Katrina to support recovery efforts and help to establish the Mississippi Community Foundation.

The recommendation sparked discussion among the congregation and an overwhelming majority embraced the call. He became the congregation's first African-American pastor. A life-long Disciple, Jackson graduated with honors from Butler

University in Indianapolis and from the School of Divinity of Duke University. His Doctor of Ministry degree is from United Theological Seminary in Dayton, Ohio, and he has received four honorary degrees. As the beloved pastor of the Mississippi Boulevard congregation, he brought phenomenal growth to the congregation in a nineteen-year pastorate.

Dr. Jackson and his wife Tina, an early-childhood educator teaching at Brooklyn College, have one son, Cullen O'Neal, who continues to live in Memphis. His ministry is providing a "fresh start" for both pastor and congregation for renewal in the new century.

Alvin Jackson's stimulating preaching reflects his heritage in the Black tradition and combines impressive charisma with sound biblical, contemporary, and socially conscious observations. Celebrating the congregation's human and cultural variety, Jackson often speaks of the "divinity of difference" as a hallmark of the church. Committed to growth in every area of church life, he is a catalyst for new and creative projects. For example, using resources saved through the years in special escrow funds for building maintenance, the church facilities have been remarkably renewed. Especially helpful in visually relating to the community has been the installation of large, open glass doors from the street to the nave. This, combined with the daily opening of the sanctuary for prayer and tours, creates a welcome never before achieved. An elevator in the Adams building now effectively removes the barrier of steps to any of the facilities.

Many new staff positions recommended by Pastor Jackson are served by outstanding personnel. Creative contributions from associate pastor, Katherine Kinnamon, include worship leadership, adult education, and supportive ministries to children, with the elders and deacons. Katherine shares membership development ministries with the other associate pastor, Monte Hillis. Monte greets and nurtures visitors in membership development. Katherine integrates them into congregational life and mission. The team is producing significant membership growth and involvement. Both counsel and nurture a team of seminary interns: Miriam Martinez, serving the Saturday Community Lunch Program, and Jennifer Crumpton, supporting the young adult ministries through the new XY 20s-30s group. Media expertise by Bill Weber produces an array of visually engaging interpretive materials and an impressive new look for *Forward*. Experienced general manager Ray McGarrigle's accomplishments are strikingly evident throughout the building. Assisting him is able facilities director, Ron Silvers. Nelly Perez, senior administrative assistant, helps to organize it all. Other staff energies are provided by controller, Adella Attalla, and long-time, efficient financial secretary, Joyce Clevenger.

In 2008 Paul M. Vasile, minister of music, a 2001-graduate of the Eastman School of Music, virtuoso organist, pianist, composer, and choirmaster, was chosen by a musician-search committee chaired by Estella Pate. He began making bold strides in enhancing the always spirited worship and arts life of the church. A growing choir, a concert series, a new youth chorale, a gospel choir, and a fledgling drumming group all attest to new beginnings, fostered by his deeply committed ministry. The popular improvisations that were a signature of predecessor McNeil Robinson continue excitingly in Paul's organ and piano offerings.

Dr. Jackson brought extensive organizational experience to the church. Governance, having been streamlined in the 1990s with a smaller official board and departments, now reflects a growing trend among congregations and is made up of a nine-member Ministerial Council with task force teams appointed for specific purposes. Even the church's name has been condensed; reflecting its lovely green neighbor, and with the pastor's encouragement, it is simply called "The Park."

Congregational growth is Pastor Jackson's passion. The diverse educational opportunities, theological inquiry, spiritual depth, ecumenical and interfaith emphases, and community programs that have long been associated with the church exhibit new energy and variety. Especially hopeful is the reconciling effort he has brought to the alienation experienced between the congregation and some of the Hispanic, African-American, and Haitian Disciples congregations of the area. His leadership experience in the international mission of the Disciples has brought recognition to the congregation and broadened its horizons. Although Pastor Jackson modestly characterizes the church's ministries as "bumbling and stumbling" their way forward, however it is achieved, this observer sees vital and faith-filled "divinity of difference" energy at work throughout the congregation and the wider community.

Another milestone is reached and passes by. The saga of two centuries of "seeking justice, embracing diversity, and inspiring imagination" is just cause for celebration. But it is only one more milestone on the faith-and-hope-filled journey. Living in and with the nation's metropolis, *The Park* – Park Avenue Christian Church (Disciples of Christ) — will endeavor to embrace, and seek to fulfill, the promise of John's revelation that with God "all things will be made new."

Afterword

Nietzsche's dark comment on existence, "What is life but a prelude to death?" an oft-repeated definition of contemporary life, has been overturned again and again by this never large-in-numbers but huge-in-heart congregation. Like the mythical, burning phoenix rising from its ashes, the people – sometimes only a remnant, but constant and faithful to the resurrection story so central to their Christian heritage – "girded up their loins," went to work, prayed, and prevailed.

Their engaging two-century saga has been barely recounted in this telling. Progressive and committed to their calling, the congregation will likely never be like the massive "lump" of dough described in Jesus' insightful parable (Matthew 13:33), but ever the "leaven" that transforms it into the "bread of life."

Always struggling to swim through the fluctuating tides of metropolitan life, the congregation has faced and overcome daunting challenges time and again. Hope is at the center of Paul's trilogy of faith, hope, and love. History is a collection of hopes – hopes dashed, hopes delayed, hopes fulfilled. The story of the Park Avenue Christian Church reflects each of these. Reinhold Niebuhr wrote, "Nothing worth doing is achieved in our lifetime, therefore we are saved by hope." Hope has been the God-inspired, vital force that wrote this story. It will always be so. As *The Park* congregation stands on the threshold of their third century of faithfulness, may their story continue to be an inspiring prelude to life on the future's ever broadening journey.

As Pastor Alvin O. Jackson began a 21st-century ministry at the Park Avenue Christian Church, he creatively coined the defining phrase, "divinity of difference," describing not only the contemporary congregation, but also encompassing its history since an intrepid group of nine embarked on a mission in William and Sarah Ovington's home in 1810. Even then, diversity and openness were the hallmarks that distinguished the Manhattan settlement from nearly all of the other more rigidly Puritan New England towns settled by the British.

Often overlooked is the fact that Manhattan Island and the surrounding territory had been a vibrant, thriving Netherlands community long before the English became dominant. Russell Shorto, in *The Island at the Center of the World*, asserts, "The Dutch Republic's policy of tolerance made it a haven for everyone from Descartes and John Locke to exiled English royalty to peasants from across Europe. When this society founded a colony based on Manhattan Island, that colony had the same features of tolerance, openness, and free trade that existed in the home country. Those features helped make New York unique, and, in time, influenced America in some elemental ways." That spirit – at its best faithful to the neighbor-loving and justice-centered gospel of Christ – has, again and again, pervaded this small, yet often audacious congregation for two centuries.

It is intriguing to note that when the congregation found a new home 70 years ago on Park Avenue, they discovered that the entrance to their handsome, landmark church was emblazoned with the coat of arms and motto of the City of Amsterdam, EENDRACHT MAKT MACHT, "In Unity [or concord] there is Strength," which is also today the logo of the Reformed Church in America. The now century-old, French Gothic-inspired church had been built by likely the first (1630s) congregation ever established in Manhattan, the Old South Dutch Reformed Church. What an irony that the construction of what would later become the home of one of the first Disciples congregations anywhere was the sad cause of the bankruptcy of the Old South Church that affirmed the strength of unity, but ceased to exist in 1912.

This book has been about the diverse folks who with sturdy faith and stubborn grit brought us to our bicentennial in 2010. Countless unnamed saints could not be included, but without them no history would have been made. With pioneering spirit they sought to fulfill their mission in light of their call. Unified in strength by the "divinity of difference," the people of this faith-filled community are the heirs of an impressive heritage. By prayerfully continuing to invest compassion, diligence, and resolve, they will ever embrace a bold future under God.

Historical Note

This text, while recounting and expanding on the 200 years since the congregation's inception in 1810, is not intended to replace, but to expand on the church's three other published histories, each of which reflects the priorities of the era of its writing and authorship. These are:

Christie, Robert, *Historical Sketch of the First Church of Disciples of Christ in New York City,* New York, 1910.

Starratt, Rose M., *A Sesquicentennial Review of the Park Avenue Christian Church New York City,* private edition of the Bethany Press, St. Louis, Missouri, 1963.

Russell, Ota Lee (principal researcher and writer), *Crossroads 175, Twenty-two Eventful Years 1963–1985,* privately published by the Park Avenue Christian Church, New York City, 1985.

Copies of each may be found in the archives of Park Avenue Christian Church in New York City and also at Disciples of Christ Historical Society in Nashville, Tennessee.

Acknowledgements

Although most of the members will recall my asking them question after question, there are those who thoughtfully responded with descriptive letters, interviews, and collected memories. Especially do I thank Allen Harris, Becky Hebert, Ima Jean Kidd, Sarah Mook, Elaine Cunningham, Jo Ann Ashley,

Wayne Reed, Juanita Shacklett, Richard Sturm, Suzanne Webb, and Jean Wirth. Special appreciation also to Ima Jean Kidd, my New York connection for detailed searches into the depths of the archives. Every reader will join with me in thanking friends and colleagues who added insights and information, each eagerly taking to heart my request for candid commentary and gladly pointing out every infelicitous word or phrase: my literary editor wife, Jensene Godwin Payne; scholar-historian Duane Cummins; publishing expert David Mitchell; and Presbyterian pastor colleague, David K. McMillan. To one individual, who has been my colleague and friend for more than thirty years, Dr. Richard E. Sturm: for the hours he sacrificed from his extremely involved life in reading, suggesting revisions, and additions from his own extensive writings, I am overwhelmingly grateful. I am especially indebted to the scores of individuals who throughout the 20th century and beyond lovingly edited *Forward*, most often a weekly record of the congregation's life and work.

Gratitude is also expressed to the Disciples of Christ Historical Society in Nashville for offering their Polar Star Press imprint to publish the book: to President, Glenn Carson, who oversaw the project; Archivist Sara Harwell, who invested several weeks organizing the scattered and jumbled materials; and to editor, Kristin Russell, who tirelessly redacted millions of word-processed bytes into a book.

While today my wife and I reside in Alva, Florida, where I serve as a volunteer pastoral partner to our minister, the Rev. Glenna Tibbs of the First Christian Church, we continue to cherish *The Park* as our New York home. Many thanks to our other pastor, the Rev. Dr. Alvin O. Jackson, for graciously encouraging me to take on such a pleasurable task.

John Wade Payne

Bibliography

Books:

Boyd, James Penny, *Triumphs and Wonders of the 19th Century: The True Mirror of a Phenenomenal Era*. A. J. Holman and Co., Philadelphia, 1899. (p. 123, tribute to Elizabeth B. Grannis)

Brewer, Urban C., *The Bible and American Slavery* : a discourse delivered at the Christian Chapel, West 17th Street, New York, on Sunday evening, January 4, 1863. Collection: Samuel J. May Anti-Slavery Collection, Cornell University Library.

Brewer, Urban C., *Shoddy Patriotism:* an address delivered at the law commencement of the University of the City of New York, Wednesday evening, May 7th, 1862 (Unknown Binding).

Burrows, Edwin G. and Wallace, Mike, *Gotham: A History of New York City to 1898,* Oxford University Press, New York, 1999.

Cornebise, Alfred E., *The United States Infantry Regiment in China, 1912–1938*. Jefferson, NC: McFarland, 2004.

Cummins, D. Duane, *The Disciples: A Struggle for Reformation,* St. Louis, MO, The Chalice Press, 2009.

Dunlap, David W., *From Abyssinia to Zion, A Guide to Manhattan's Houses of Worship*, New York, Columbia University Press, 2004.

Foster, Douglas Allen and Williams, D. Newell, *The Encyclopedia of the Stone-Campbell Movement,* Erdmans Publishing Co, Grand Rapids, MI, 2004.

Janvier, Thomas, *In Old New York,* New York, Harper and Brothers, 1894. (Republished by St. Martin's Press, 2000.)

King, Moses, *King's Handbook of New York City*, Moses King, pub. c 1890.

Kurlansky, Mark, *The Big Oyster: History on the Half Shell,* (History of the City of New York), New York, Random House, 2006.

Payne, John Wade and Jensene Godwin Payne, *A Grace of Seasons,* (Excerpts from Sermons, Communion Prefaces and Prayers), privately published by Park Avenue Christian Church, New York, 1999.

Payne, John Wade, Rosenberg, Roy, Meehan, Peter, *Happily Intermarried, Authoritative Advice for a Joyous Jewish-Christian Marriage.* New York, Macmillan Publishing Co., 1988.

Russell, Ota Lee (principal researcher and writer), *Crossroads 175, Twenty-two Eventful Years 1963–1985,* privately published by the Park Avenue Christian Church, New York City, 1985.

Stanford, Elias B., *Origin and History of the Federal Council of Churches of Christ in America,* Hartford, CT. S. S. Cranton and Company, 1916.

Starratt, Rose, *A Sesquicentennial Review of the Park Avenue Christian Church New York City*, St. Louis, MO, The Bethany Press, 1963.

Tucker, William E. and McAllister, Lester G., *Journey in Faith: A History of the Christian Church (Disciples of Christ)*, St. Louis, MO, The Bethany Press, 1975.

Periodicals:

Campbell, Alexander, ed., *The Christian Baptist*, 19th century periodical.

Campbell, Alexander, ed., *The Millennial Harbinger*, 19th century periodical.

The Christian Evangelist, early 20th century periodical, published by the Christian Board of Publication of the Disciples of Christ, St. Louis, MO, various editors.

The Disciple, Disciples of Christ 20th century periodical, St. Louis, MO, various editors.

DisciplesWorld, www.disciplesworldmagazine.com.

Errett, Isaac, ed., *The Christian Standard*, 19th century periodical. (Continues under different editors.)

Forward, periodical newsletter of the Park Avenue Christian Church, New York City, published since 1899.

Homily Service, published by The Liturgical Conference, Silver Springs, MD. (Homiletical resources from sermons by John Wade Payne and others, 1990–1999.)

Shepard, Silas E., *The Primitive Christian*, periodical published 1835–1841. Troy, New York.

Other Resources:

Bates, Miner Lee, *Outlook and Appeal,* Centennial Convention Report (1910), W. R. Warren, ed. Delivered October 16, 1910, Luna Park.

Brooks, Rachel Gleason, *The Chinese Sunday School at the Disciples of Christ Church.* Archival paper, Park Avenue Christian Church. 1928.

Christie, Robert, *Historical Sketch of the First Church of Disciples of Christ in New York City,* New York, 1910.

A CURIOUS CHURCH CASE, "A STAR CHAMBER Church investigation, published for a warning against Pharisaical Hypocrisy, which, above all other sins, Christ condemned. ELDER ROBERT CHRISTIE, AIDED BY DEACON FRANCIS M. APPLEGATE, Induced the Official Organization of the Congregation of the First Church of Disciples of Christ, in New York City, to 'WITHDRAW THE RIGHT HAND OF FELLOWSHIP' FROM ELIZABETH B. GRANNIS, 46 Years a Communicant and Member of this Congregation, BECAUSE She withheld her sympathy from its Pastor, Rev. B. Q. Denham, while he was under six months' trial in a Criminal Court in New York City for Indecency. . . ." Harvard University Library, April, 1910.

Henry, Frederick A., *Isaac Errett's Contribution to our Movement,* Centennial Convention Report, W. R. Warren, ed. 1910.

History of Harrodsburg (KY) Christian Church:
www.HarrodsburgChristian.org

History of Manhattan Church of Christ:
www:ManhattanChurch.org

Bibliography

History of Park Avenue Christian Church:
www:ParkAvenueChristian.com

Idleman, Finis, *Tent Dwellers of Faith,* lecture to the Disciples of Christ Commission on Christian Union, Chautauqua, New York, July, 1919.

Idleman, Finis S., *The Alpine Glow,* The Spiritual Resources Committee, 1930.

Idleman, Finis S., *Peter Ainslie, ambassador of good will,* New York, Willett, Clark & Co., 1941.

In Memoriam – William Jackson Jarman. Published by Park Avenue Christian Church. 1978.

Philputt, James M., *Christian Unity,* an address at the Centennial Convention, 1910, W. R. Warren, ed. Delivered Sunday morning October 17, 1910, Duquesne Garden.

Sturm, Richard E., *Conclusions on the History of our Northeastern Region and the Future of the Christian Church (Disciples of Christ).* Presentation to the Northeastern Region.

Willett, Herbert L. 125th Anniversary of the Central Christian Church, New York City, October 13, 1935: Willett, Herbert L., *Anniversary Address*, Tributes to Finis and May Johnson Idleman. Title page: *The Chancel of Central Church of Disciples of Christ, New York City.* Privately published by the church. 1935.

Windows of Opportunity: Reflecting our Past, Framing our Future. The Restoration of Park Avenue Christian Church. Booklet containing summary of the project by Walter Melvin and Charles DiSanto, architects and the names of contributors to the various phases of the work. 1994.

Archival Material:
Disciples of Christ Historical Society, Nashville, Tennessee.

Museum of the City of New York

The New York Public Library

The New York Times, New York, NY

Park Avenue Christian Church, New York, NY

Finding Guide

Most names and organizations listed are found on multiple pages throughout the book. The page numbers are, generally, the first reference.

To learn more about the
history of Christians and
Disciples, visit the primary
source of the
Stone-Campbell heritage

www.DisciplesHistory.org